The Lightworkers Handbook

Matthew Penn

For Sharon, the Kids,
Nan & Gramps.

xxx

Matthew Penn

CONTENTS

" Love is the plant that grows from the seed of compassion"

Spiritual development need not be a baffling process

The complexities of life can cause even more stress upon our well being than in fact the very challenges that sprout from them. This becomes more apparent when we begin our journey into spiritual development aiming to further our blossoming growth towards the pinnacle of our path.

So then the sensible thing to do when embarking on this path would be to vanquish the complex details of our physical human state of being into the steady spiritual light that will become stronger and stronger.

Spiritual development should not be viewed as some complex web spread out across many different systems, beliefs, rituals and behaviours. If we begin our journey as a child begins theirs with a curious, playful, joyful mind not focusing on the larger more grown up issues of the universe or all the metaphysical name dropping or higher wisdom which is only attained by the few.

Instead just gazing upon it with the unconditional love of being a universal child. Then a true spiritual path will emerge from our inner most being and in turn bringing us further into Alignment with our true self.

It is a fools perspective that teaches the spiritual way from behind a mask of labels and judgements. but the child like mind which guides the way to the path of truth and enlightenment.

It is a beautiful thing to begin our spiritual adventure.

"I woke this morning to a fresh new day, as I do everyday and have every morning for thirty one years, I look forward to waking tomorrow (if my path permits) to another new world just as a new born baby leaving the womb. With experiences...good or bad, Large or small. This does not matter to me as all experiences are building blocks granted to me so that I may nurture and feed my growth".

This is the only way it can be. For if not my path will simply be a mirror image of a bumper cars chaotic trip, bouncing my way through life. Good experience...BUMP....bad experience

...BUMP..until eventually there is an inevitable crash!

As you embark on your spiritual journey and even throughout your path. You will face obstacles, you will encounter challenges. Denial - Suppression - Anger - Jealousy - Judgement etc. all products of the Ego will all mould you into a bumper car mindset.

However the child's mind knows nothing of these and does not harbour or hide behind these masks.

Rediscover your inner child, learn to smile at the little things and laugh at the cracks. You cannot fix the worlds problems and should not expect too either. Just enjoy the journey and rest assured you will help many on your path which is a huge step towards accomplishing your goal as a lightworker.

What is a Lightworker?

The term Lightworker has evolved over time. Initially used to describe people who were involved with humanitarian, spiritual or healing work. As our knowledge grew the term became more associated with people who it is largely thought are at the fore front of the evolution of human consciousness. A term used often by Lightworkers is Waking up. These individuals view themselves as entering a period of waking up when they begin their spiritual journey.

But A Lightworker is not someone who is more highly evolved or further up the spiritual chain than anyone else. They are not more susceptible to the unseen forces or have any other special privileges than those around them. We are all Lightworkers in a sense of where we are from and where we are going. However those who use the term Lightworker are aware of this, they are aware of who they are, the path they are on and the direction they are taking. Most often in life (in fact all of us) We are born and are raised by our parents or guardians.

Their influence as well as life's circumstances, situations, friends, challenges and the influence of our colleagues often moulds or shapes our personalities and pathway into something that simply isn't our true self. This is OK and is not a major issue for most. This is the automatic pilot most of us live our lives as.

But a Lightworker is someone who is waking up to this knowledge or Fully aware. That the Life they have been living is not in line with their True self. This waking up can become apparent via a sense of feeling. They have a purpose or set goal in life that perhaps isn't being fulfilled and other symptoms. Many Lightworkers feel they have some sort of mission... However discovering this can be quite daunting, confusing and even scary for some.

Each and every person at some stage will be given the opportunity to wake up and re align with the true spiritual nature of them self. To take up their role as a Lightworker.

When someone wakes up to their spiritual path it is like a heavy burden becomes lifted, clarity comes into their life once more and a sense of purpose will encompass their future goals. Being a Lightworker can sound like someone who has bridged the gap between them self and the divine leaving others behind.

This is not true though we are all connected to the divine it is simply that Lightworkers have an awareness of their true self. A Lightworker will walk in this light with compassion, love and knowledge as their tools. Walking the path of wisdom and compassion is the spiritual way and this is a Lightworkers driving force. Their path is always aimed at the highest good of all, without judgement or ego driven fantasy. The Term Lightworker is not a label that should be used to hold influence or power it is simply a term used to express and define the individuals who choose this way of life.

Remember we all have Free Will and choice

Being a Lightworker is certainly no difficult task when down on paper. In fact it is a very simple one. But as with most things in life it is the ability to continue and follow through where the challenge lies. Lightworkers face many difficulties and challenges often a their path can be fraught with negative instances or obstacles. It is viewing these circumstances as challenges that need to be over come in order to fulfil their path and move on that gives the lightworker a sense of control over self and their journey. switching off the auto pilot and no longer living out pre prescribed roles laid down by others. This will begin to bring them back into alignment with their True self.

A Lightworker needs also to be open and aware that there are many spiritual beliefs and practices in the world that have been granted to us. To belong to one is lovely but there is no need to be anchored to any one system or practice but rather view them all as gifts or tools that we can utilise when working towards our goals.

Spreading Knowledge, joy, compassion, love, kindness, warmth and Light! This is the role of the Lightworker and Lightworkers are needed to wake up now during these times.

Waking up

So are you a Lightworker? Is anyone you know a Lightworker? Being a Lightworker is not something you can train to be. You either are or you are not and that's it. It doesn't matter its just either your time to wake up or not. There are some simple signs and symptoms you can look out for to answer this. You can begin to feel bodily aches and pains. This is not something to worry about it is simply the intense changes that are occurring around you and within.

You may have a very up and down emotional state. At times feeling a deep inner sadness for absolutely no real reason. The ups and downs of other peoples emotional traumas can have a deep effect on you and leaving you feeling quite drained or even useless to their plight. Other times the little things in life can easily gift you a wonderful lift. A colour, animal, glance from another or simply seeing joy. Your sensitive nature will put you very much in tune with the world around you.

There is also a pull or a compelling nature to help where you can. So much so it may look to others like your interfering or being a bit of a busy body. Lightworkers are drawn to helping others and this pull can often lead them into situations, where perhaps they should have stepped back and thought should I get involved? And this is perhaps one of the elements of a lightworkers personality that needs to be kept in check at times.

When waking up to their spiritual path Lightworkers will be drawn to seek out knowledge. This is a major factor of their waking up and also an essential element to their spiritual growth. Its probably the very reason you are reading this Handbook and will read many more. A thirst for knowledge can be an overwhelming desire for a Lightworker and unless they can fulfil this desire their minds can become a little stagnant and this is where loss of direction can step in.

If we do not seek out the truth, the knowledge that will enable us to live out our life's mission then lightworkers are in danger of becoming depressed and seeking other avenues to fulfil this need. As strange as it may seem if they do not follow this direction they can often be found turning to alcohol, drugs or another desire or addiction. Many lose their way through poor teachings (overly confusing development courses or structure), giving up, never seeking this in built desire for spiritual growth and instead replacing it with false desires that never truly make one happy they simply replace and fuel material need. Lack of support, peer pressure or ,many other reasons the fact of the matter is that when one is drawn to seek something more, this should be pursued rather than passed by. This is your opportunity!

As a lightworker enters their period of waking up they can encounter problems with sleeping, eating and are bombarded through their five senses repeatedly. This is a perfectly normal encounter and can be a very exciting time. All sorts of experiences are shared amongst lightworkers, many of them similar although it is also important to remember that no two experiences are the same.

Every bodies waking up period can be expected to be very different and this is one of the elements that can make this such an exciting time. When I was waking up I was actually quite scared by it all initially (well if im honest for quite a while). I was working nights as a Lorry driver when my experiences became shall we say enhanced. I had always had a spiritual side. Spent most of my life searching for a spiritual path, Christianity, Buddhism, shamanism. I had an interest in many, in fact I actually got quite deeply involved with some.

However I always felt it was never enough. There was something missing. It wasn't until I met my partner who explained her views on spirituality and introduced me to certain areas of spiritualism that things began to really speed up.

What once were boring nights driving my lorry from place to place delivering all on my lonesome to car service stations became a Ferris wheel of magic and colour. Although there are many energies working with us throughout the course of our day, for a lightworker emerging from the cocoon working nights alone was actually an ideal situation for me. There was no running away from it and no ignoring it. Something was changing.

These experiences ranged from seeing spirits, hearing them, strange encounters with animals and some signs and messages which I was able to validate later on. It was scary at times however as time went on I did come to the realisation that nothing is going to hurt me. This was a development process I had opened my self up to and if I closed it off now I would miss out.

I hardly slept during this period, my eating was very up and down, my ears would ring at times (and this became more frequent), my eyes were seeing flashes of light and colour and this became more of a fixture that I just don't worry about now. Information would flood into my thought process, I knew things I wouldn't dream of knowing! Where did this information come from? Gradually I became aware that this was all coming from my guides and higher self. More importantly I had a strong desire to do something with my life. The feeling that something important was coming and that I could help in some way and even more so the feeling of connection to every single thing animated or inanimate. There was a strengthening link there.

If you are waking up to your path you can expect to have similar experiences I had many but everyone's development process is personal too them. And This is not a book about me its about you.

Types of Lightworker

Lightworkers come in many forms and it is very possible that a lightworker will not even go through this period of waking up to the extent of others. Some people already go about their path as a lightworker. Striving towards the good of all and the higher good of the planet in their daily lives. Simply because they want to. They don't know why they just have a desire to help. An inbuilt yearning to serve. These people can be found in many different professions the obvious ones Like :

- Doctors

- Nurses

- Paramedics

- Firemen

- vets

Lightworkers can be fulfilling their roles in other ways though completely un aware working as :

- Musicians

- Artists

- Aid workers

- carers

- gardeners

and of course there is many more.

Food for thought :

spend some time looking at the job section of the paper and see what jobs you think would equate to a lightworkers role. Try not to look at the obvious and see how a lightworker could be going about their business completing their mission without even realising. One role for instance could be the humble street cleanser.

Although this is not everyone's job of choice there is much reward to be had from cleaning our streets. It is a service to others and to the planet. When we view it as such the importance of such a role can equal or even surpass other more commonly favourable positions.

So Lightworkers can be found by their professions. But of course we do not all get to take up the job of our dreams and so we go about our life path doing what we can in other ways. This can make meeting other lightworkers quite a difficult process as at the end of the day they look act walk and talk just like everyone else! So there really is no specific type of person instead it is the inner characteristics of any given individual that makes them a lightworker in this life time. You will meet people who will suggest that they are a Lightworker and will begin to point out that they are some highly evolved individual who has vast knowledge on the metaphysical aspects of life blah blah blah. I'm sorry to burst their bubble but you will find these people are not lightworkers at all but rather use the label as a method for their over inflated egos to take a platform. A Lightworker will not act in this manner. Humbly focused soley on the service of the universe and world around Ego driven ideas are not part of their characteristics or personality traits and this demonstrates the fine line between Lightworkers and name droppers. It is very important we do not get caught in the trap of following this path.

Your higher self and the contract

One of the things that many people have difficulties in understanding or facing up to is that you are not you. You are not the human version of you that you have become so accustomed to. You are a spiritual being in essence and the real you is a perfect version of you living in the ether. So lets just take a moment and look at that. When people say (and this is a term you may hear bounced around a lot) The ether, where are they talking about? Its a common misconception by many to feel the ether is some place in the far reaches of space, miles up in the sky like heaven. The ether is all around us, its everywhere, but the reason we cannot see it is because it is on a different vibrational frequency to us. One way to think of it is to think of radio signals or T.V signals. They are everywhere yet we cannot see them... but we do know they are there.

The thing with being in the Ether is that it is not a physical realm. If we need to travel or perform an action all we need to do is think it and its done. Its quite a baffling subject and we will only touch on it briefly but one way to think of it, is that we are all made up of energy and what we are seeing now is the physical result of this. Just as we do with light, we do not see the light with the naked eye all we see is the by product or after effect of that light – the reflection. The ether is the realm of frequency where the energy swirls round in an intelligible mass. Also known as the divine energy. So what we are here in our earthly realm is a projection of this energy, a projection of our true self, the spiritual being of energy. So our True self resides in the ether and remains in constant contact with us. From the moment we enter the womb however we become contaminated by our human existence, our physical form. No one is to blame for this, it is as they say life.

From birth we listen and learn from those already in the world. We learn from our parents, our friends and our colleagues. The media plays its part, music, cartoons, films, games everything and as we grow we pick up information from the world around us. This is how we learn right from wrong, and the people who teach us learnt that from their parents etc. Its like a vicious circle of absent minded teachings.

We cannot blame any one because its no ones fault, the human race simply lost it way and so we teach as we have been taught. The older we grow we gradually drift further and further from our spiritual self and the connection becomes weaker. All your higher self, (your True self)can do is guide you from the other side, whether you listen or not its still your choice.

So why are you being guided? Before we are born into this life and are existing in the ether as a perfect intelligent spiritual being we have the opportunity to undertake different life paths or life journeys. This is what you are on now your current life path. As we know everyone's life here on earth is different, different experiences and different trials and tribulations. What we do (and this may sound crazy at first) in the ether is we choose to undertake certain life paths in order for us to learn certain lessons.

So yes you chose this life, you only have yourself to blame. When we decide to undertake a life path we have a binding contract which we sign regarding the path. We also assign A Guide to help us. This is generally known as your central guide or chief guide, we will discuss more on spirit guides later. We have our contract and we have our life path and so we are born and from the ether (with the help of other spiritual beings) our higher self sets out to guide us through the many lessons we face and ensuring we fulfil our life's contract.

As Lightworkers we seek to realign ourself with our higher self and this means leaving behind a lot of what we have picked up during our earth walk and returning to our more spiritual state of being.

Bringing our self back into alignment with our higher self is very good for our well being. It brings in a state of balance and harmony to us and benefits us on all levels. This really is not a difficult process for us and is a lot easier than some would say. All we need to do to begin the process is spend some time getting to know the physical mass we inhabit.

Our bodies. We do this on an intimate level. Noticing signs and messages that our body is telling us then once we have this intimate knowledge of how our body feels we then work towards maintaining it through our thought process. It is very simple. All the feelings of our body stems from our thoughts, negative or positive. When our body feels out of balance or a little off , we are not in line with our thoughts or higher self.

Think of it this way when we are going through times of great joy and celebration we do not stop and think we must be in alignment with our higher self. An inner knowing of well being, a flash of inspiration or stroke of genius. This is us being in alignment with our higher self and our body feels good because this is the projection of this, the mirror image. Our body is a mass of sensitive areas and it is through learning to notice the state of how our physical self is that we can see how much in tune with our higher self we truly are. It really is that simple.

What do we do? Well when see sense or feel some form of discomfort within our physical body meditation or some other relaxation process will bring us back into alignment and this need not be a difficult process :

- Light some incense or candles if they help you relax and play some meditation or other relaxation music if you wish

- lay back and get comfortable

- Relax and surrender yourself fully to the moment allowing your thoughts to drift in and drift out not forcing anything just going with the flow

- As you do this in your mind ask your higher self

" what is my body trying to teach me"

and just allow yourself to sense the answer. This could come through feeling, tasting,sight or sound you may even smell the answer. It all depends on the situation. You may find that your intuitive side steps in and boom the answer just comes to you.

- Spend time doing this, do not rush, stay in the moment until you have answered the questions you came in with.

This is a great way to begin sharpening and honing your intuition. The more you do it the stronger your intuitive side and your connection to your higher self will become. You can do this for anything. Questions regarding your future, work, love life absolutely anything. The more open you become to your higher self the more information will flow.

You see it is not that hard all you have to do ...is ask.

The Mission

What is the mission? Well ultimately global peace and unification. But the thing is as an individual that task does seem pretty out of reach and highly unlikely. One man cannot save the earth just as one women cannot bare all of its troubles. This is not your mission. The chances are you are not here to restore world peace and change the universe. What you are here to do is the little things. Its the little things that will work towards the greater outcomes. It is those deeds we have an opportunity to perform on a daily basis which are truly commendable and productive.

Again this is so simple, forget all the shift in cosmic energy stuff and this is our time of global alliance piffle (which is always banged around on the internet) Forget all of that, its irrelevant, unrealistic and a waste of your thought process. As a Lightworker you are here to serve and make a difference to the lives that you can. Your family, friends, neighbour, colleagues, the homeless guy you see everyday or the people in the residential home up the road. This is where it begins not on some far fetched intergalactic mission that seems purely to serve ego.

Again I am bubble bursting but it needs to be said. For Lightworkers to truly make a difference and fulfil their mission they need to accomplish what they can. You can take the time to help an old lady with her shopping, you can go to the park and pick up litter, you can volunteer some time at the homeless shelter and you can ensure that anyone who comes into your presence leaves feeling happy and has a desire to share that joy.

This is what its all about and through such actions you can cause a chain reaction. The old saying a smile is contagious holds an awful lot of weight here. So don't just read about it and especially don't just talk about it, in fact don't even mention it just get out there and do it.

The Three Paths

To assist a Lightworker in furthering their development and spiritual growth I have laid out three paths to follow. The path of awareness, development and compassion. If we can learn to build on these individual pathways we not only have a firm foundation for further development but we will also be in far greater attunement with our physical self, our higher self and the world around. Which is a definite plus. They are not a difficult practice. You will find things in amongst the three pathways that you will see elsewhere in a much more difficult often confusing way. This Development programme is simple and highly beneficial when adhered to and practised throughout our life path. Please also remember there is no right or wrong way. Only the way that works for you. The instruction that I put fourth in this Handbook is a guide line. If you stray a little from this don't worry. It will not affect your spiritual growth and all will happen as and when it is supposed too.

The Path of Awareness

One extremely important factor when we begin to wake up to our spiritual path is becoming aware. People often think that we must focus soley on the metaphysical aspects or developing their psychic self. This is a huge misconception and to be honest will only hinder your development. To fully develop and further our growth we first need to be aware of what is going on around us in this realm. This is where any actions we take or decisions we make are largely affected and so it is clear we need to know what's going on around us and within us. Through raising our awareness of the here and Now we are beginning on a journey known as present moment living or mindfulness.

Mindfulness is a beautiful practice which originates in Buddhist teachings. It allows us to learn to live in the present moment rather than dwelling on the past or focusing on the future. Remember that what has past has past and thaws not happened yet is irrelevant also. The only moment in time you actually have any power over is this very second. This moment, and it is through this awareness that present moment living emerges. Not only does this practice allow us to have a calm mind free of worrying or stress related factors but we also have an opportunity to sharpen are five senses. Many people over look these when beginning their development and this can also often be the very reason that they fall at the first few hurdles. To build a solid foundation in spiritual growth we need to heighten our awareness.

The very first thing I would like you to do is clear all blockages of negativity . Remember this is spiritual Development. Love and compassion are the driving force. Any negativity or bitterness towards anyone is simply going to delay your process. Become of a mindset : I have many people in my life who have really hurt me. Keeping hold of this emotion doesn't change that or make it feel any better. If it does this is simply an illusion caused via the ego....Let it go and understand it is not my place to feel the need to punish them with negativity, the only person I am punishing with this ultimately is myself.

Exercise

So how do I begin to do that?

Write a Letter to yourself !

Dear ....,

I know that 'Kate' hurt me and betrayed me but I will not allow her to consume me. I acknowledge these feelings and understand them however now It is time for me to release all of my feelings towards her, be them positive or negative. If ever a thought of negativity about her should arise within in me I will immediately acknowledge this feeling understand it and then release it. She does not control me or my feelings or actions. I allow only positive people into my inner most private space. (now sign it)

THEN

Write a letter to her (but don't send it)

Dear 'Kate',

Although you hurt and betrayed me I am sure you are going through your own inner struggles and thus I am releasing the pain you caused me. I wish you peace and happiness because if you don't find that then the only person you are hurting is yourself. I acknowledge the feelings I have towards you however I choose not too allow them to consume me.

Then sign it.

If possible burn the two letters as a release...if not then rip it into tiny piece releasing all negativity.

This is not going to be a quick fix because you will still hold anger and bitterness but whenever it creeps in simply acknowledge and release it because keeping it allows him/her to take away from the good and positive things and ignoring it simply causes suppressed emotion which will only surface later.....

2. Now take a cleansing shower (a real shower) and as you shower..... imagine your old self being washed away and down the drain. Any hurt or pain let it wash off you and watch it go down the drain. Once you get out and towel off you will tell yourself you are ready for your spiritual self to emerge. Go to bed with a paper and pen and write down each dream you have. You may have to continue to do this. It is OK to do it every time you shower as it is a great tool.

Becoming mindful

Mindfulness is a very simple practice indeed and yet it is one of the most difficult to sustain. Why is this ? Well largely due to the world around us. In today's modern busy society we simply complain and moan, worry and stress. Our minds are like a run away train of speeding emotions and thoughts going round and round like they are on loop de loop.

Its quite amazing actually that it isn't until you actually stop and think (no pun intended) that you realise how over active your mind and thought process is. We are not talking about becoming mindless robots either with no thought process. Your not going to build a vacant mind, walk around dribbling or become and emotionless soul. You are going to become aware of what is going on within your thought

process and emotional state. There are millions
of books on this and it is not over complicated
and does not need to be confusing The trick to
raising our awareness is keeping it simple.

When we are little babies and we first set out to
learn how to walk we will have fallen over
numerous times. So much so this would stretch
into the hundreds possibly thousands. But the
thing is we never give up. We try and try again
until we grasp the difficult task of putting one foot
in front of the other while maintaining balance.
We find this second nature now but back then it
was a huge task and this is the way we must
look at our spiritual growth and personal
development. As we have come of age we have
built up layers and layers of thoughts, emotions
and automatic triggers due to the influence of
our parents, friends, work colleagues and the
media and also from the various circumstances
and situations we encounter.

Setbacks are part of the process of spiritual
development and personal growth. These will
affect our confidence and anxieties. Its only
natural. However they do need to be faced
acknowledged and dealt with in order for us to

make any solid progression. From this point I would like you not to look at setbacks as Negative situations but rather a learning opportunity. They are not failures, they are lessons granted to us in order for us to learn, move on and pass this knowledge onto those who walk the path behind. When a setback occurs simply get up and try again but do so with a smile if possible.

When our confidence needs a bit of a boost and there are anxieties towards working with people or spirit.it is beneficial to look at bringing some mindfulness awareness into your daily routine.

simply put mindfulness is purposefully paying attention to our present moment with three key elements :

- Acceptance
- Compassionate
- Curiosity

When we live in a state of awareness we are living in our present moment and the beauty is this present moment can become an enjoyable experience for us because worrying about the past or concerns for the future do not come into play.

It is the art of Learning to **Be** instead of Learning to **Do.**

From a simple perspective the past has already been so this cannot be changed and the future...well that hasn't arrived yet...so this is completely unknown and any thoughts on this are pure speculation.

The only moment you actually have any power or control over is Now. This moment is where you can make decisions, think, act,listen and create any paths that ultimately will bring in future journeys.

Meditation is a key element to this practice . Mindfulness meditation is a particular type of meditation that can be carried out anywhere and any time. There are five key factors that we focus on with mindfulness meditation :

- Our breathing
- Our senses
- Our body
- Our thoughts and emotions
- whatever is in the fore of our awareness

There is one other key element to remember with meditation

There is no wrong way to practice

There is only One way, which is your way. So when practising meditation please do not ever come out of it thinking that didn't work as it should or I couldn't follow that meditation. These are all **Judging the meditation experience** which will only impair your experience. View your meditation as it was and whatever occurs during your meditation accept simply because its personal to you. Even if you fall asleep or cant get in the right mindset just accept it as it is and move on with your day.

This is what mindfulness is all about – Acceptance its not focused on fixing the problem its focused on accepting the problem and change may come to the situation or it may not come later. So when it comes to Anxieties or stress about things Mindfulness will show you how to accept these feelings and through this acceptance change will follow as a natural occurrence.

Acceptance means acknowledgement it does not mean giving up!

Do this now.....

- Put the book down where ever you are

- Close your eyes and breathe normaly

- Watch your breathe in with the positive.... and.... with the negative

- feel the breathe in.....and ...out

- Allow any thoughts that come into your mind to flow not stopping on them just let them pop in and pop out until you can bring your attention back to the breathe. It doesn't matter if thoughts distract you, just acknowledge them and continue with the breathe

- In .....and ....out calmly at your normal breathing pace.

- how does your body feel? Feel all the sensations your body is giving you

- are you warm, cold, tired, aching, do you feel good? Where are the sensations?

- ⅢⅢⅢⅢⅢ them and continue with the breathe feel complete oneness with the breathe

when your ready Bring your self back, open your eyes and look about you

This exercise need only take 2-3 minutes. All your doing is allowing your mind a chance to come back to the here and now, to check in with your body and slow that thought process down. For that 3 minutes you were in the present moment. Not allowing your thoughts to carry you away on an emotional roller coaster, the white knuckle ride of stress and upset. You were complete, in this moment just you and your life breathe. You will find that if you have a busy job at the computer all day or any job to that matter if you place a little reminder at your desk or in your home that reminds you to breathe and every time you see this you carry out that short meditation your day will become easier and in fact will be more productive.

Remember also you do not need to stick rigidly to this, there's no right or wrong way. Your just taking a moment to check in with the here and Now. You can make the meditation longer or shorter you can even listen to the sounds around you allowing your ears to pick out what's going on, what's important is your focusing on the breathe and being in that moment. Not allowing your thoughts to bog your down. They come in...they go out Like a natural flowing river rather than a Tsunami of thoughts.

What I would like you to do is just spend some time observing your thoughts over the next week. Being aware of our thoughts is not difficult but throughout life we do grow into a series of Automatic paths of thinking, we have learnt to associate our thoughts with our own identity.

But we are not our thoughts and You are not a robot

You are not a robot, you are a spiritual being and your brain functions as a whirly gig of thoughts and emotions constantly. What you are learning to do is not become a slave to this automated process. Recognise the thoughts and feelings that come in. This is what we mean by acknowledgement however don't allow them to become you. They are not you. They are simply a bi product of the every day events and occurrences that we struggle with throughout our life path.

When we see an incident or a situation that would come across as sad for example a bird struggling to fly, when we see this and we feel sad we are experiencing the emotion of sadness. We do not become sadness in that instant yet we fall into the trap of stating I am sad.....your not sad you are experiencing the feeling of sadness. As your awareness grows you will realise that the many thoughts and feelings you encounter are not you, they are experiences and should remain so. We do not become the experience we observe and learn from them.

We do not become unemotional either or discard emotions and thoughts as something that is not our own because they are, we just realise that the emotion is something we feel and experience but it is not us. I am not sad – I experienced the feeling of sadness.

Extending our practice of awareness

now you have managed to bring your self back into the moment in a simple and enjoyable way that can be carried out anywhere, we shall look at how you can become even more aware. One of the times we often find our thought process running away with us is when we are carrying out every day tasks. Now when your washing up, cleaning the car, eating your dinner, driving, doing the kids homework with them etc. it isn't practical to close your eyes and be in the moment. Of course not because then you wouldn't be in the moment you would be taking your self off and away from the present job at hand. So to live in a state of awareness, in the present moment when we are carrying out these tasks we learn to focus on them. For if we are not and our mind is thinking of other things like bills, what's going to happen Monday, that guy at work who really ticked you off etc.

This is not good for our state of mind and well being as a whole. Not only has a detrimental effect on ourselves but also on our family life and work life. Isn't it a fair enough point that when we are busy with the kids we are actually busy with them and not allowing our mind to wander else where? And the beautiful thing with this is we realise we are back in control. You do not see these situations as others are taking up your time while you should be doing this that and the other. Instead this is your time your, your in control and you have power over it. Thinking about other things holds no consequence over the current moment. You are not giving up time but rather your being in the moment not allowing time to be your ruler.

The Cup of Tea

Most of us have a favourite beverage which we like to have when we take a rest, get up in the morning or before bed. Be it Tea, coffee, hot chocolate etc. we say to ourselves "im going to have a nice cup of tea before I wash up". The thing is already your thinking about what's coming next. As the kettle boils we are looking at the sink thinking ugh ill do it in a minute, as we put the tea bag in we may think " I thought John was gonna wash up" as we stir it and take our seat we may think " ill have to be quick before I have to pick up the kids". At what point there did we focus our attention on the very thing that was meant to give us a bit of relaxation time...the tea itself. So we were never truly making a cup of tea, we were busy thinking about what's not happened taking us out of the moment and unaware of the magic which was occuring in the cup under our noses. The sight, sound and smell of the rewarding brew.

Exercise

You deserve a break! Put the manual down if your able or when you can and make your self a nice soothing drink. Lets say for the purposes of this exercise it is a cup of tea, but it can be what ever your taste buds fancy.

- As you fill the kettle and turn it on, grab yourself a cup choose which cup you wish to use. IF the cups have different colours choose one which appeals to you.

- Make your tea as you like it milk, sugar etc. what shape is the tea bag round triangle square? As you fill the cup feel the warmth rising and notice the beautiful patterns that the steam makes. Allow this to carry the fragrant smell of the tea to you.

- Breathe it in hold the cup up and savour the smell. What does that smell remind you of ? Think about this as you carry it to your chosen seat.

- So here you are in a seat that you chose with the cup of your choice filled with your

favourite beverage. As you take a mouthful
don't just swallow or gulp it down. Allow the
taste to fill your senses. How does it feel at
the back of your throat. Grow a curious mind
with your tea. Thinking about where it came
from, all the hard work it took to get to you,
the man hours that worked so hard for you to
have this moment.

• Someone worked very hard for you to enjoy
  this Tea.

• Savour every mouthful and spend this time
  focused soley on your tea, if any thoughts
  come in about anything else allow them to
  but don't focus on them simply acknowledge
  them and let them go. This is your time with
  your tea.

This is what we do. Every task we are
completing at the given time becomes the most
important task in the world to us. There is
nothing else at that point in time apart from what
we are doing. Easy on paper but very difficult to
sustain at first. As you go through your day start
by picking out things that you are going to do in
a state of awareness. Like today im going to :

• Wash the dishes in a state of awareness

• Do the ironing in a state of awareness

- Eat my dinner in a state of awareness

You can start by picking one task a day and then gradually incorporating more until you feel you can pick one day a week which will be your day for complete awareness.

A day of Awareness

choose one day where you can be completely in the moment. You know you will not be bothered by anyone its just you and your development process. Lets say you pick Sunday. Right yourself a little note and place it where you will see it first thing in the morning as a little reminder.

This is your day of awareness. When you see this reminder (which can be anything remember this is your day) in the morning before you even rise lift a half smile, close your eyes and breathe...in with the positive....out with the negative....totally aware of this moment tucked up in your warm bed ready for the day to begin. Lovely, open your eyes and have a big stretch. How did you sleep ? How does your body feel today? Feel every muscle as you stretch off and make your way out of your bed.

As you go about this day try to do everything in a state of awareness, brushing your teeth, going to the toilet, etc. Try and make this day, a day where you don't have to go out. Its just you and your state of awareness. Run yourself a nice bath, complete some jobs around the home, relax and do some gardening. It doesn't matter as long as you are taking the opportunity not to focus on other areas of your life or other days all that matters is this day and what you are doing. If you do have other thoughts come in to your mind that's OK just acknowledge them and let them go bring yourself back to the current moment.

At the end of the day write down in a journal all your experiences throughout the day, how you felt, what emotions came up to you etc. Keep this journal going now throughout your development as writing things down not only helps us to express emotions but it is a great way to validate things that occur or may not make sense at the time, however when we look back on the occurrence all fits into place.

The Path of Development

We are all granted a number of tools that allow are given to us to assist us throughout our life path. And by learning how to develop these you will find some very wonderful new doorways opening up to you. Suddenly what once may have been quite a dull world has a new perspective.

Psychic development seems to be the new rock and roll these days. As you surf the internet there are thousands of courses, books, DVDs, cds, groups, associations and webs sites that speak of higher transcendental metaphysical piffle paffle. Which is OK for some but mind boggling to others.

I used to be one of these people who like to discuss all the metaphysical fluff that's floating around using really long words that only make sense to the privileged few.

Then my eyes were opened. When I started to teach people spiritual development I realised its not that hard and that everyone can develop these gifts. Which is yours for the taking not some thing kept aside for more highly evolved individuals.

What we will do together is learn various forms of developing and strengthening your connection to all the spiritual forces that are around you. There is nothing for you to fear and everything will happen at the pace it is supposed to for your development. Please don't worry about making mistakes or getting it wrong as there is no right or wrong way here. Don't let your development end there either. Look for new teachings and ways you can communicate. Be open to new ideas and suggestions. Tunnel vision will get you no where.

Grounding and Protection

The very first aspect we will discuss and possibly the most important one is what we call Grounding and protection. Grounding and protection is of the up most importance and it is the one thing that should be practised regularly and correctly throughout your development process and beyond. However this does not mean it is not simple.

What is grounding and protection and why do we do it?

Grounding and protection are what keep you safe and balanced when we are working with the spiritual world. There are different energise that we encounter throughout our lives. Some positive, some negative. We like to welcome the positive energise but it is good practice to protect our selves from the negative ones. So where does this energy come from? Energy is a completely neutral substance. It starts out life as neither positive or negative. It is actually us who personalises it. It is how we use this energy that makes it into what it is. Lets say I take some energy and direct it at someone towards their higher good, this would be viewed as positive energy. However if I did the same towards someone but without their highest interests at its root this would be negative energy.

It is these energise that we need to protect against. There is positive and negative energy busying its was around the universe and this our world on a constant wave of chaos. Every time we have a thought, emotion or carry out an action we are building energy. We may not see it but it is there.

Lets say for instance you someone cuts you up in their car on the road while driving to work. Your first reaction may be to swear or curse at the driver of the other car. In that instant you have created negative energy and sent it out into the universe like a shock wave. When we view it like this we can actually see how irresponsible it is to act in this manner.

All this negative energy that is blasted out daily gathers and has to go somewhere. But to put the shoe on the other foot imagine what it would be like if it was a huge mass of positive energy encircling the cosmos? Now there's a thought.

Grounding is when we ground ourself to the earth ensuring that we remain in this moment in time, in the here and now and keep those feet firmly on the ground. When we are not grounded or in connection with the earth we can feel unbalanced and a little lost. Being Grounded allows us to think more clearly, feel safe and secure and you can actually communicate with the spiritual realm more productively. So it is equally as important as protection.

How can we be sure we send out positive energy?

- Stay in touch with our weaknesses and allow ourselves to grow towards a healing nature

- When we see other people it is important to see the positive aspects to their personality

- Feel compassion towards ourself and the rest of the world

- always be prepared to see things from another's perspective no matter how indifferent it may seem.

- Lose any judgemental aspects of our personality

- Be honest with ourself and allow others to do the same

- Share any negative thoughts or emotions (this is not the same as blasting them out)

- Allow yourself to celebrate and rejoice in the success of others

- when you feel fear persevere, never give up

- Plant the seed of dreams and allow yourself the opportunity to see your visions through

When are we not sending positive energy

- when we ignore our weaknesses (this can lead to denial)

- When we focus on the mistakes and downfalls of others

- focusing our time and energy on becoming perfect or our perfections

- not allowing the perspective or point of view of others

- Trying to please others constantly ignoring nurturing our own needs

- allow the moods of others to direct and dictate our own

- suppressing negative thoughts and emotions (they will only rise again at some point when least expected)

- Being resentful of others

- Ignoring our goals plans and dreams for the future

The Awareness practice we spoke of earlier can help you with this as will the path of compassion that comes later in the Handbook.

Lets Ground and Protect

When ever we embark on any spiritual practice where we are opening up energy we need to take a moment to protect against negative energy and Ground ourselves. All you need to do is :

- close your eyes for a moment and relax

- slow steady natural breathing..in ...out

- Breathe in positive energy and out with the negative

- As you do this just visualise a white light coming down from above and engulfing your entire body. Feel its warm loving positive energy

- As you watch this light move down your body towards your feet visualise some roots growing out from the souls of your feet and into the earth.

- These roots go way into the ground and you can feel a strong sturdy connection to the earth

- Gently open your eyes and know you are grounded and in a safe protective light of divine energy.

Thats it. Simple Isn't it. A simple enough practice that many forget to do. There are other ways we can Ground by simply Drinking plenty of water or a personal favourite of mine Walking or sitting bare foot in nature.

Another way to protect is visualising that you are putting on a protective coat full of colours like an armour. You wear this coat throughout your day and if your in a hurry just call your Angels and guides in via your minds eye. They will never let you down.

Meditation

Meditation is the key to any form of spiritual growth and development. It has become clinically proven that meditation will help with many problems that we face in today's rat race society. Yet many people will still shy away from the idea of meditation thinking of it as some airy fairy hippy concept or strict monk doctrine. This is not the way to view meditation at all. In actual fact it is a simple practice that will allow the sitter to re connect with themselves and the energise that flow around them.

This can be done in a simple sitting three minute meditation at home, While walking through the park, waiting at the bus station or relaxing in the garden. It really can be done anywhere contrary to popular belief. There is no set right or wrong way either.

You do not need to fold or bend yourself into some great yogic position, candles and incense are not a necessity and neither are singing bowls or the beat of the shamans drum. Sure these can be tools that some people find helpful to bring themselves into a certain state of relaxation but they are not essential.

Meditation can bring calmness and inspiration to your world, but it also allows you to take control over your spiritual senses. When I first started meditating, I strongly assumed that I could master it overnight..... who wouldn't? Truth is that I found laying down more comfortable than sitting and used to practise lying on my bed....and then ended up snoring my head off until the early hours of the morning.

This was frustrating until I learnt it really didn't matter that was the experience of the meditation. I never actually mastered meditation overnight! Not that it is difficult..... it just requires discipline and lots and lots of practise. No one ever masters meditation, but it is worth the effort... . In order to discover your spiritual gifts you need to broaden your awareness first and be able to let go of everything that holds you tight before you commence on exercises that increase your spiritual ability.

Remember where possible :

- Wear comfortable loose clothes when sitting
- Make your surroundings as clean and comfortable as you can
- Don't meditate in a room where there

have been negative energies because
of recent arguments or a   room
where you are likely to be disturbed.

- Switch off phones

What is meditation ?

The ability to meditate is the ability to journey
within oneself. When we meditate the aim is not
to sleep, levitate or bring our mind into a vacant
state. Far from it. The aim of meditation is in
actual fact to be in a state of high alert. When we
meditate we are observing our body and our
thought process. We allow our selves to ride
along a river of calm and tranquillity allowing the
answers to be bought to us rather than us
chasing them.

In order for us to connect with and receive
guidance from the higher realms our thought
process needs to be slowed down and
quietened. This is so that we can allow our
connection to the higher realms to strengthen. Its
like being on the phone in a crowded
environment, we have to find a way to quieten
the surrounding noise in order to hear the voice
coming through the receiver on the phone.

We do this either by walking into another room or telling everyone to shut up. Taking ourself out of the noise is normally the preferred method and this is all we are doing with meditation. Your not telling your train of thought to shut up, no as this simply causes suppression of thought or emotion (when we do this the suppressed thought or emotion always comes back at a later point) your taking yourself to another room, another level within ones self so that we can receive the messages from our body and higher self with clarity and direction.

As we go into meditation we focus initially on our breathing. Do not change the pace of your normal breathe behaviour. Not too deeply, not too long or too short, calm steady rhythmic breathing as you would do normally. Trying to breathe to a count or in a particular fashion would not allow the meditation to flow because you are controlling too much.

Meditation is also about no expectation, when we expect a meditation to be to a certain standard or have a particular outcome we are not allowing the practice to flow. Just remain normal and breathe calmly, softly and gently...in ...out. Its impossible to relax if we force the breathe in anyway. Calm natural breathing is required for a calm natural meditation.

What follows is a meditation to set you on your path. Please do not worry about sticking exactly to the meditation itself, all meditation is personal to the individual participating and all guided meditations should be viewed simply as guidelines to help you along. What you should be doing in essence is allowing your meditation freedom to explore and receive the answers you seek. As you Progress through the Handbook you will have more meditations applicable to the specific practice or subject.

Observing the body

This is a meditation designed to keep you in touch with what your body is telling you. It is very important that we listen to the little messages our body gives us on a regular basis and this meditation is a lovely way for us to begin our Practice.

Before any meditation complete your protection and Grounding first!

- Make yourself comfortable laying down or sitting with your arms resting gently ext to your body.

- Close your eyes if you wish (contrary to belief this is not essential however does make the process easier for most)

- Allow any thoughts that come in to come in acknowledge them and let them go

- Breathe, gentle calm breathe with a steady rhythm....in with the positive...out with the negative....

- as you breathe and when your ready feel your body becoming more relaxed feel the sensations in your body, from your toes, knees, fingers, stomach, chest, shoulders and up towards your head.

- Check in with your body. How does it feel? Aches, pains, comfort,discomfort,What is your body telling you?

- Accept these sensations and Analyse the entire scope of your physical form

- Now visualise a beautiful pure white light coming in to your body through your crown

- Allow this light to fill every joint, muscle and bone slowly coursing through your body

- feel its warmth and energy

- Allow this energy to heal and rejuvenate your entire being

- Spend some time with your sensations and experiencing your body

- When you feel the meditation has come to an end bring yourself out, shake off, have a little stretch if needed and return to your day a rejuvenated spiritual being.

Simply Meditate anyway,anywhere, any time

How was that meditation, did you feel it went well? Cont worry if you feel it didn't as all meditation goes exactly as it is meant for you at that time and the only thing you can expect is that it will always be different. Just remember there's no right or wrong way. You can meditate anywhere. Those times when you are sitting and find yourself gazing at a spot on the wall and your mind drifts freely. This is the time you can meditate. Allowing the mind to calmly flow without force, stress or strain. When your at work at your desk, just stop, breathe, focus on a spot in the room and allow the stress of the day to flow away. Bring your mind back and move on. It only takes a few minutes and you will find your productivity increasing, it really is that easy. This is taking a little time and its essential for your spiritual development. A calm mind is a productive mind.

Chakras

The chakras are best thought of as vortex's that are at certain points on the surface of our physical body that allow divine energy to flow through. There are a large number of minor chakras but Seven major ones, which is what we will be focusing on. The word chakra itself comes from Sanskrit and means either Wheel or turning.

They are constantly spinning like a fan and are thought to be the central points for retrieving and transmitting energy. The chakras themselves are invisible to the human eye. But you will find that there are many different drawings or paintings depicting them as flower shaped or wheel like gateways. These images vary Depending on the Belief system that you are working on. Either way they are very real and present no matter how we depict them.

The Seven major chakras are energy centres that you can find running along the spine. These positions are set, they do not change their location. They are in positions from the base of the spine to the top of the skull. Chakras are connected to our aura and to understand them we must also look at the aura and its role. The aura is a field of energy that envelopes the human body. This energy is working in connection with our chakras and has seven different levels : Etheric, Emotional, mental, Astral, Etheric template ,Celestial and ketheric Layers.

Why maintain the chakras and The aura ?

The importance of maintaining the chakras and the aura is paramount when we are embarking on our spiritual development and throughout our daily lives. This is fundamental to our well being on all levels and you will reap the benefits from this very soon after initiating energy maintenance. Just like a car goes into to be serviced regularly we must do the same with our energy source and portals.

Our chakras are the Key to balancing the energy that passes through the aura and into our being. They are also the points that send out messages in the form of energy from us. These are influenced by our emotional state and physical well being. So as we discussed earlier about positive and negative energy these are the gateways for what gets through to us.

What we strive to do is keep our aura and chakras in a state of balance. We first need to know when we are out of balance and this is a simple process. Simply by observing ourselves and our reactions. Which brings us back to awareness. When we are aware we can pick up on these emotions.

What does each chakra do ?

1 . The root

The root chakra otherwise known as the base chakra is the first chakra and Is located at the bottom of our spine. This is associated with the colour red and is linked to the etheric Layer of the auric field. Its main function is Grounding and survival. When we balance this chakra we will help to improve and maintain our overall health and give the physical body an energy boost.. Often linked to the Planets Earth and Saturn as well as the stones Garnet, Ruby, Onyx, and Obsydian.

2.The sacral

The Sacral otherwise known as the Naval chakra is the second chakra and is located in the Lower abdomen. The sacral is associated with the colour orange and is connected to the Emotional layer of the Auric field. Its main function is to do with our desires, pleasure and sexuality. When we balance this chakra We are maintaining our sexual vitality, fertility and our physical power. The Planet it is linked to is the Moon and the stones coral and carnelian.

3.The Solar Plexus

The solar Plexus chakra is Located above the Naval and is associated with the colour Yellow and is connected to the Mental Layer of the Auric Field. The main function of the Solar Plexus is dealing with emotions such as Anger, happiness and our willpower. Laughter is a fundamental aspect of the solar plexus. The solar plexus is linked to the planets Mars and our sun.when we Balance this chakra we are affecting various aspects but mainly it is a source of calming allowing us to ease our tensions and stress. The stones associated with the solar Plexus are Amber Topaz and citrine.

4.The Heart

The hear Chakra is located in the centre of our chest and is associated with the colour green. The Heart Chakra is connected to the Astral Layer of the Auric field. This is the chakra that's main function is Love and compassion. The Planet that this chakra is linked to is Venus and its stones are Rose, quartz and Malachite. This chakra is very important for our circulatory system also affecting our compassionate side and loving energise.

5.The Throat

The Throat chakra is Located in our throat area is the colour blue and is connected to the etheric template of the Auric field. and its main functions include our ability to communicate as well as our creative urges. A Place of ideas. The colour associated with the Throat Chakra is a Bright blue and its planets are Mercury and Neptune. A well balanced Throat chakra is important for our speech and the way in which we communicate.

The stones that are associated with this chakra are Agate, Blue Lace, Sodalite.

6.The Third Eye

The Third Eye Chakra is located in the centre of our forehead Directly above the eyes and is connected to the Celestial Layer of the Auric field. This is where our inner knowing and intuition come from. The colour associated with this Chakra is Indigo and its planet is Jupiter. The stone associated with this Chakra is Lolite. This is the chakra we need to balance to assist us with our Psychic intuition.

7.The Crown

The Crown Chakra is Located in the very top of our skull and disconnected to the Ketheric Layer of the Auric field. Its associated with the Colour violet and the planet Uranus. This chakra has an affect on all our psychic abilities as a whole, also rejuvenating and bringing vitality. The stone associated with this Chakra is Amethyst. This is the chakra that restore our inner state of bliss when balanced.

Balancing the Chakras

When our chakras are out of balance you can visit someone who is an energy practitioner and who is skilled in manipulating the energy flow and balancing chakras. This can take more than one appointment and could also be costly depending on where you go. you can balance them yourself and can keep your chakras in a nice healthy state of balance and never needing to seek assistance from a outside source.

Balancing Chakra Meditation.

- Ground and Protect

- Make clear your intention " I am going to meditate with the intention of balancing my chakras"

- Breathe a calm steady normal breathe in....with the positive...out with the negative.....in.......

- Continue your breathing at a slow steady pace until you feel totally relaxed

- Visualise Each chakra

- See and feel their powerful spinning vortex focus on each one for as long as you can

- One by one from root to crown

- the longer you can focus on each chakra the better the outcome

- Bring yourself out of the meditation when you are ready

This is one simple technique. Another great way to balance our chakras is Yoga and the use of crystals. The important thing with the meditation is that when you go into it you are clear with your intention. " I am meditating now with the intention of balancing my chakras.".

Remember if you cant visualise the chakras this is not a problem it does not mean the meditation has not worked, visualisation is simply an aid and the more you mediate the better at visualisation you will become.

To Maintain the chakras we can :

1. Make use of a proper diet – When we feel we are out of balance or our chakras need re alignment eating healthily will make a huge difference. Take a look at your diet recently you will be surprised what a difference a little change can make.

2. Exercise – yoga, gym, aerobics or perhaps partaking in a refreshing walk in the country. Any form of exercise is a great way to keep us in balance.

3. Giving our house a cleaning blitz – our outer world is often a mirror image of our inner state of being. Take a look around your home and living space. A brisk clean up a de cluttering of our home can have the same affect on our chakras.

4. A Revitalising bath – Having a warm relaxing bath with scented candles or other tools which help you relax. While there close your eyes and bring yourself into a gentle meditative state, calmly breathing and allowing your body to unwind itself.

5. Chakra Stones – Having the chakra stones we mentioned earlier on about you or on your person can also help to maintain balance.

Working with Energy

Energy is all around us an within us. Like a web pulsating around the universe in constant motion. We can train our eye to see this energy and also to manipulate it for certain tasks when they are directed towards the highest good. One thing we need to be clear on is that all things are connected by this energy and this energy emanates from all things. Whenever we enter an area or leave an area we leave an energetic fingerprint. We cannot stop this occurrence and we cannot force it, its simply there for all living creatures. Animals, birds, insects and humans. Every thought, intention, action or misaction will leave your energetic finger print. Positive or negative energy its your choice but either way it will remain. This is why it is wise to think before we act.

When people begin working with energy it can be a difficult process at first. The old saying seeing is believing comes to mind. What people cannot see they very often dismiss far too early and so the final result becomes vanquished by the negative response they have with dismissing or non belief. You have to believe when working with energy. If you do not have full faith in what you are doing, that subtle hint of non belief is enough to out way the original intention. Belief and patience is needed.

If you don't believe in what you are doing it wont work and if your looking for immediate results then you'll luck out too. All work with energy or spirit should be done without expectation and with faith that what you are doing is for the highest good. Everything happens for a reason and if its going to happen it will at the point that it is meant too for your spiritual growth and development. So please be patient.

Seeing the Aura

One of the simplest exercises we can learn is seeing the Aura. This is a great way we can tell how someone's sate of being is, mood, health etc. It is a gradual process and the eye does need training for it. As your vision becomes stronger you can expect to be able to see the first two possibly three Layers of the aura quite quickly. Most people can only ever get to see the first two layers. So please don't threat or panic if you feel nothings happening and progression halts at two. Seeing one layer is pretty awesome stuff.

All Living things have an aura. This includes trees. When you have an opportunity of a clear sky at night make your way outside and find a tree or even a plant that stands alone with the sky behind it. Sit down and make yourself comfortable. Bring your mind into the calm meditative state of steady natural breathe. Look at the very tip of the tree and gaze upon it allowing your mind to clear, its just you and the Tree.

As you gaze simply allow your eyes to come out of focus and try to hold this. The longer you can hold this gaze the better although at first it may be quite difficult. Notice that there is a white Hazy light now surrounding the tree and coming up from its tip, this is the Trees energy field. The more you train your eye like this gradually you will see this energy going right up into the night sky like a channelled flow of energy from the divine. You can practice this anywhere any time its easier at night at first but the more you practice the more you will see.

Try it on your hand. Find a white background or peace of paper and place your and in front with your gaze around 20 - 30cm away. Just as you did with the Tree. Calm meditative mind and bring your eyes out of focus. You will see the initial hazy white glow and the more you practice you will begin to see colour coming into the glow. This is the human aura.

Try it on friends, family, pets and have fun with it. Every colour of the aura has a different meaning referring to your physical, mental and spiritual state. Each colour also has a different density. The Lighter and clearer the colour the more positive, when the colour is murky and muddy the more negative.

A brief over view of some of the colours you may see

Red

Red is the colour of passion and power. Money worries, obsessions,anxiety and forgiveness.

Orange

Orange is the colour of energy, stamina and an adventurous nature. An outgoing personality but can also be a sign of addictions.

Yellow

Yellow is the colour of inspiration. Being creative playful and an easygoing chilled out state of mind.

Green

Green is the colour of comfort and nature. Representing a time of growth and balance.

Blue

Blue is the colour that represents the desire to care for and assist others. A sensitive colour also representing our intuitive side.

Violet

violet is the colour of magic. Sensitive and wise this colours is seen when there is vision and scope.

Grey

Fear and potential health problems

Black

Unforgiving normally on a long term basis. Entities attached to the aura, health problems and grief.

Sending Healing

As a Lightworker you are probably drawn to healing others as best you can. Many people join groups or take up courses in healing when they feel this pull and this is great. Its a wonderful thing to be able to offer healing to someone when it is needed. The important thing to remember with healing is that the energy you utilise is not from you. Many people work with healing fall into the trap of claiming the healing energy comes from them. This is their ego growing a little to big or they have been give misinformation. Healing energy comes from the divine and we simply channel this energy for its purpose. In no way shape or form is the person conducting the healing responsible for the energy that was channelled. The credit for this goes to the divine.

Hands on healing, Reiki, shamanistic healing and other practices should only be completed once a sufficient level of competence has been reached under professional instruction. There are many courses available for this.

One thing we can do however is send positive energy as a form of distant healing to an individual or incident. This can be very powerful indeed and should not be over looked. If you feel someone you know could do with a little positivity it is always best to get their permission first so they are receptive to it.

- Ground and protect

- Bring yourself into the calm meditative breathing state

- breathe in with the positive....out with the negative.......

- Once you feel a state of calm focus on the individual in question

- Visualise this person standing before you

- See a beautiful white light coming down from the divine and allow it to envelope this persons energy field

- watch as its warm glow comes down upon them as you do this feel the love in you reaching out to them and being received into their sacred space.

- Smile and allow them to share this smile, all you can feel is positive warmth and love towards them.

- Stay with this for a few moments and then steadily bring yourself back

Energy Balls

Another way you can send someone loving healing energy is via an energy ball or psi ball. This is very simple to do and a quick method of sharing a wonderful, positive, healing energy.

- Ensure your hands are clean Ground and Protect

- rub them together as if your trying to create static energy between them

- now slowly bring them apart so there is space of around 10 – 15 cm

- close your eyes and feel the energy between your hands and finger tips

- you will feel like a pressure this is the outer rim of your energy ball

- Gently ring your hands closer together until you feel the pressure is quite firm like your holding an invisible ball of energy

- Say " I am filling this energy ball with love and positive healing energy".

- Then open your eyes, raise your hands above your head and throw the ball in the general direction of where that person may be

- Don't worry if your not sure it will get to themselves

You can do this as often as you like, just ensure that you ground and protect prior as with all things when working with energy and spirit. After a time you will be able to see the energy just as you can the aura which is also great fun to practice and learn.

Spiritual Assistance

We are all granted assistance on our path from the spirits that are around us and watching over us. The thing is though we often lose our connection or become unable to receive the messages they offer purely through growing up. Children have the wonderful ability to see and hear spirits, we often watch our children joyfully playing on their own and chatting away to themselves totally unaware that they could be communicating with the spirit word.

Why is this? Why do children have this ability and why do they lose it as they grow?

We are born into this world completely untouched and uncontaminated by ego or influences. As we grow we become more and more contaminated, this clogs up our receptive capabilities and so we lose that wonderful connection. A child has a curious mind, everything is new and fascinating, it is this experience of the new that allows a child to be inquisitive where grown ups just walk on by, they notice the little things.

Their minds are not full of worries and stress. Their minds are free to roam and receive information. As a child I had a invisible friend. His name was diddy. Everywhere I went diddy went and people always laughed at me and my imaginary friend and they still do today. The amazing thing is though I can still remember diddy, I remember what he looked like, I remember him always being around and if you saw diddy you would not think of this person as a child's imaginary play mate.

Oh no, diddy was an elderly man, he had long hair on the sides with a bald spot on top. A brown waistcoat, long white socks and baggy brown pantaloons tucked into them. With a white (Feminine looking blouse). Diddy had tired , sad eyes never spoke but was always there.

I feel that if diddy was an imaginary friend I would have chosen someone a little more colourful and fun! More to the point if diddy was imaginary why can I still remember what he looked like?

Diddy was a spirit plain and simple. I don't know now what he wanted and perhaps never will. Perhaps I am mentally ill ? Or perhaps he was a spirit who was just there so I would remember him today and so that I could tell you my experience. So when you hear of a child with an imaginary friend. Before you laugh about it or dismiss it perhaps it would be a good idea to take a closer look.

There are many kinds of spiritual beings. Some were once human others not. Some are helpful and again others not. It is important when we are learning to connect with spiritual beings that not every single one will have your best interests at heart. This would be a foolish notion. It is best we learn how to connect to the ones who will hold our higher good in the greatest of esteem rather than the more negative beings.

Relations

One of the things most people look for when they embark on spiritual development is communication with loved ones that have passed. We all like to think that we are being watched over by our loved ones and this also leads to a lot of disappointment if we don't manage to communicate with anyone we once knew. This is very common and as I have said before please do not go into this with pre conceived expectations or hope.

what many people do not teach or are afraid to say is that most of our relations move on after death. They begin a new path or are assigned to watch over someone else. One thing we have to make clear at this point is each of us resides in the ether as a spiritual being. When you return there your not the person you were during your period in physical form on earth. You return to being a spiritual being. Your family on earth are not necessarily going to mean the same to you once you are in the ether. Because In that realm emotions take on a different perspective. The pains, upsets and obstacles we face during our time here do not have the same affect on us in the spiritual realm. There is no pain, emotional attachment or upset. These are the reasons we take up our life path in order to experience these.

To the extent that if you were to meet a relation in the Ether you may not have the exact same relationship as you did on earth. This does not mean your relations didn't love you or don't once they cross over, its just a completely different realm and state of existence.

This is just the way it is. It is important that we are aware of this so we do not build up expectations. With this in mind however it is not always the case. Most of us do have one or two relations in the Ether who are assigned the task of watching over us. Largely for familiarity. We can be more receptive to spirit if we feel we are talking to a loved one or an acquaintance we once knew.

This may be hard for people to swallow but unfortunately this is largely due to the attachment we build up in this realm. When mediums connect to People who have passed and we are under the impression that our relative is in the room, they can see and talk to them as though they are a solid person I don't see this as the case .I feel What they are actually doing is picking up on the spiritual energy of that person. Their spiritual finger print. Other spiritual beings will help them to do this (Like our spirit guides) in order for the sitter to receive the message needed.

Another misconception is that our relatives become Angels. Angles are not humans and humans cannot take Angelic form. They are two completely separate beings and they cannot become one or the other. So the best thing to do is not to expect or go looking for a connection with a loved one or relation with the thought that they are now an Angel. If a relation comes through for you then that is truly wonderful and should be a treasured moment if they don't, please don't become disheartened it just simply isn't meant to be. There are some wondrous, loving, caring spiritual beings who have their main focus on you and your life path just waiting for you to open up to them.

Spirit guides

We all have spirit guides that are watching over us on our life path. Every single person on this planet has a central guide assigned to their life path before they are brought into the womb. This is an arrangement that has been made between your higher self and the guide in question. These highly evolved spirits are your very closest companion. Their love for you is unyielding and their main focus is on you completing your life path and fulfilling your life missions as outlined prior to your birth. Your central guide will be with you from the day you are born until the day you die. They are not with you constantly however and you are not the only person they are watching over. They step in at various points when needed or when they are called upon.

So what is a spirit guide?

A spirit guide will have lived many human lives before and so has become highly evolved and learnt many lessons in order to guide and assist people now. They can take any form they wish and offer messages to you of guidance and support in the way most receptive to you. So our work with our central guide is a very personal one. As we grow we can even find ourselves being drawn to things in our lives that show aspects of our guides personality. This can happen without us even being aware of it. A draw to a certain country – could be a link to our guide, A draw to a certain job – could be a link to our guide and even the way we look – could be a link to our guide. When you begin to venture into this path it is truly amazing the more you discover about your guide you will discover about yourself and find reason behind many likes, dislikes and aspects of your personality.

Your central guide will also at times call on the assistance of other guides who will come in to help you with certain tasks or areas of your path. These guides may just come in the once to do their job, they may be around more often or throughout your path depending on their role. These guides may seem a bit more work orientated and not as open to building a relationship as your central guide. The simple reason for this is that they just come in to complete a certain job and then go again. There very busy beings you know and wont always be in a position to hang around for chit chat and a cup of tea! So if a guide comes through for you and they seem a little stern don't take it personal because it isn't They simply have a job to do.

By learning to reconnect to our spirit guides we are opening a doorway that will help us to make excellent progress on our spiritual path. Our guides will help us to develop our spiritual gifts and abilities ensuring we can reach our full potential. This is of course only if we are receptive and open.

How do we connect to our Spirit guides ?

Communicating with our guides really is not a difficult process for you to master. There are many books and websites that will lay down some complicated ritual or another that promises you communication with your guides which only turn out to be an over complicated mess. Think about this statement " Your guides and Angels are there to assist you and are awaiting for you to communicate with them......why would they make this a difficult process?" the answer is they wouldn't. That would be totally out of their interest and yours. They want you to communicate with them so that they can assist you as they are supposed to in a full and comprehensive way.

We are actually already communicating with our guides constantly only most of us are unaware of it and our guides don't mind. They don't seek recognition as long as their job gets done. An example of how are guides are working with us is that sense of knowing that we get but often cannot explain. We know we should take some form of action, we even here a little voice that says in our mind don't do that, that's Wrong matt or It would be more appropriate for you to do this.

Now you'll notice that when I heard the little voice in my mind it spoke to me in the third person. Saying my name Matt rather than me or im. Because it wasn't me it was my guide. It is very easy to miss largely due to all the traffic buzzing round our mind making lots of noise. When we Calm the background noise we can receive the messages clearer. Some call this your conscience others your inner voice. Either way it is your guides communicating with you. That voice doesn't just come from anywhere and think about it logically if you were advising yourself you wouldn't call yourself by your name or in the third person. So listen to your inner voice.

There are other ways in which we can communicate with our guides. In fact we can even meditate and journey to meet them in their plain of existence and have conversations with them. As well as offering us messages throughout the course of the day, protection and of course love. They ensure certain elements come together on our path when they are supposed to in order for us to complete our life's mission. A surprise invitation, chance meeting, turn of good fortune all leading to a key point on our path. Were these coincidental or orchestrated?....this would be between you and your guides.

Get your note book and Try to ask your guide 1 question every morning (write your question in this book) as you go through your day write down any signs which may answer the question you have asked. You need to pay close attention to everything around you… it may come in a song, road signs, telly or through a friends actual words. You will feel in your heart that this 'sign' is just for you. Here is a story that might explain it better… when I met my partner she started introducing me to ways that I could contact my guides… I asked for a white feather as confirmation that I did indeed have a guide with me.

On my way home on a busy road a white feather drifted onto my windscreen in plain view. And as I started developing my gifts and opening up to the spirit world, I was unsure if I was indeed connecting to my guides and asked for confirmation, I then drove past a neon sign with flicking lights stating… 'Britain's finest currently under development' This sign was there all the time.. But I never noticed until that moment I was supposed to notice.

You can also ask your guides for small favours e.g. if you are going to a busy shopping mall where you know there will be no parking… tell your guide that you are on your way to the shopping mall and ask them to make parking available to you. You can ask them to protect your car when you leave it unattended as well as your house. Always remember to thank them when they have done something for you.

If you do not get the answer on the same day, ask the same question the following morning as it does sometimes take a few days for guides to manifest answers to you. Don't ask for help to win the lottery… as I have tried this several times and they just wont budge!

Now we need to start acknowledging our guides are around us If you want to use your spiritual gifts, the cheapest, fastest and easiest way is through meditation. There is no way to skip this exercise as you will need it most of the time. Now I would like to try and introduce you to your Guides via meditation. The more you Practice the easier it will become.. Your guides will then start taking you on awesome journeys through time and space into a different universe than ours.

Meditation tips:

Don't expect too much from this first attempt, but try to commit yourself to at least 10 – 15 minutes of mediation per day.

Start Meditating:

- Put on natural meditation music and maybe light a few candles if you wish

- Shake your arms, stretch them and your legs so that you are entirely comfortable

- Find a comfortable position for sitting straight, both feet on the floor.. or just laying down (comfortable is the key)

- Try to rest your palms upward if you are laying down, or on your knees if you are sitting

- allow a calm natural steady breathe in with the positive ...out with the negative.

- Listen to your heart beat to release stress and worries

- Feel the Aura.. the energy that surrounds you

- Breath in this energy.. imagine it entering your nose when you breath in and circulating around your body.

- Continue these steps for a few minutes until you feel your body relaxed as if it were floating on a cloud. Just keep your breathe at a natural steady pace.

- Once your body is relaxed visualise the roots growing from your feet through the ground to the centre of the earth . As your roots reach the centre of the earth there is a pulsating white light that reaches up along your roots until it fills your body with Diving light. Imagine this light surrounding your body and your Aura. Once you have done this, you can move onto visualising the meditation below.

For our first meditation I would like to try the following.. Please don't be discouraged if you struggle on your first few attempts. Just keep trying and you will succeed.

Exercise 2

Meditation Exercise – Read through this a few times and then visualise

Focus on your heart-centre and concentrate on your breathing for a few moments, quietly inhaling and exhaling 'through your heart'. Ensure that your spine is straight, relaxed and comfortable, supported if necessary. Allow your normal steady rhythmic breathing to carry you.

As you go deeper visualise that before you stands a Rose coloured Temple step forward into the temple, and now you are surrounded by a gentle rose colour. Feel the softness of the interior of the temple, a wonderful place, soft to the touch,with a warmth that envelopes you.. a beautiful pure light emits from the centre a place of perfection and purity.

Step forward now into the centre…….. before you is a golden arched door, carved with ancient and inscriptions and symbols shimmer like fire these are words and symbols of great holy power and importance.

You realise that this door holds magic that leads to a wondrous world of dreams. Stretch your hands out and place them on the door.

Your spirit guides Love your hands, they view them as instruments to be used in service to others. Feel the magic and beauty of the symbols beneath your hands as you push open the door.......Now when your ready step through

For your first meditation we will only go to the door... try this meditation as many times as possible until you are able to visualize it. Don't worry if your meditation is not exact or not even close to the one given....as we are never able to control the information we are given.

Once you feel comfortable with your meditation, answer the following questions and write the answers in your notebook. The whole idea of this exercise is preparation:

- Were you able to breath through your heart easily?

- Did you see anything around you when you stood in front of the temple of Rose? Describe what you saw

- Did you see what was written on the door (symbols or words)?

- Did your hands light up?

- What colour where they?

- Did you see a dominant colour at all in the silence.. if so, what was it?

- when you pushed the door open, what did you see?

Once you are able to visualize the previous meditation, you can incorporate the below meditation...... this time step through the door and follow the below:

Now you have entered the plain where our guides reside. You are in awe at the purity being carried through the air. Breathe in this pure air filled with goodness and truth as you gaze around at the many shimmering pools of light. Walk forward. As you move forward witness all nature in its purest form.

Now you come to a pool, Kneel down by this small expanse of water and gaze at its still waters. Like a beautiful crystal mirror shimmering in the light. With the pure blue sky above you can feel the warmth of the sun on the back of your neck, you feel safe and protected.

As you look at your beautiful reflection you see a beautiful figure take shape behind you. You see its reflection in the pool, a gentle approachable wonderful face. With a smile so kind and pure.

Then an influx of colour comes in and dances across the pool like a celebration. Turn around now and face the guide who has come and see their radiance. The guide looks at you with pure love in their eyes. It is this love that your guide greets you with, you know this is your central guide. The guides eyes reassure you of this. You have a bond that is strong and stretches far back all this becomes apparent in this instance..

You allow your guide to take you by the hand and walk with them to a nearby seat. Over looking all the beautiful greenery and nature here in this special place. You feel complete peace.

Speak with your guide now if you wish, you will receive the answers to your questions.

As you do Listen to the wondrous music which surrounds you. Now Look into your heart. Your Guide has given you a precious gift…. Say Thank you to your guide for such a blessing..

When you are ready you feel a lightness coming into your body, lifting you like a feather. Peacefully and happily you are carried along a breeze of peace back through the Arched door. As you go through you are brought back down to your feet in the room where you began. You are back from the plain of your guides and know in your heart that you may return whenever you need your guide.

Bring yourself back to normal consciousness, visualise each chakra closing and ground yourself.

How did that feel? Write all your experiences in your journal. Remember the meditation did not have to go exactly as was written and don't worry if you found it difficult just relax and try again.

How else can I communicate with my guide?

You can also communicate with your guides on a daily basis using divination. Different divination techniques include the Pendulum. This is a practice largely found in spiritualist circles and other systems however fundamentally it is the same. The Pendulum is a very basic instrument which you can buy in many shops with varying crystals and chains, but you need not buy one for training or even at all. The pendulum can be made very easily. In actual fact if I need to communicate with my guides or need their assistance in finding something I use a necklace which I wear and find it is perfect. Remember when we work with our guides its not how fancy the tool as long as it does the job we intend it to do.

What can we use the Pendulum for ?

The Pendulum can be used for various purposes. Like asking for guidance to make certain decisions,for finding missing objects and even people and for healing purposes. We will cover just basic use for your pendulum but be adventurous and try using it for different things.

How To Make a Pendulum

All you need to do is attach a small medium weighted object to a length of cord around between 30cm and 110 cm long. You can use a Bolt a piece of jewellery, key ring or key, etc. it can be anything that you can find. It doesn't matter as long as its right for you. Remember your only learning if you wish to purchase a pendulum at a later date go right ahead but for now its really not necessary.

Using the Pendulum

There are various rituals you will find around the internet for charging your pendulum and I feel this really is personal preference and again not a necessity.

The pendulum swings In different directions to give different answers. The circular motion is the ready position.

When the pendulum swings forward directly in front of you this is the direction for yes

when the pendulum swings across your body from left to right this means no

If the pendulum swings diagonally to the right away from your body this means Maybe or will not answer.

The best way to work with the pendulum when your learning is to draw out a map on an A4 piece of paper like compass points with yes being at north, no running from west to east and maybe at north east.

Then you can see which answers you are being given on the paper. By holding the pendulum over the centre and allowing it to move to the answers that is offered.

Before you begin ensure you Ground and Protect.

Hold the Pendulum between your thumb and forefinger over your sheet with the answers on..

As you hold the Pendulum you will become aware that slowly it moves in a circular motion. Before you ask anything always ask your pendulum are you from the Light?

This is very important and should always be asked to ensure that you are receiving messages from a positive not a negative source. Positive will always answer yes and negatives cannot. If a negative does come through simply place the pendulum down ground and protect , ask your guides to come through for you and try again. Never entertain a negative.

Now tell your guides you would like to train your pendulum to the map you have drawn and slowly manoeuvre the pendulum around the map about an inch from the surface until you have covered the area of the answers fully.

All you need do now is Ask clear and concise questions and you will receive yes no answers. When you are learning your guides will answer practice questions as long as you let them know you wish to practice. Heres some questions to get you started :

• IS the sky blue?

• do I live in....?(where ever you live)

- Do I have kids ?

It does not matter what you ask as long as you let your guides know you wish to practice and always remember to ask if they are from the Light. Your guides want you to ask it and expect you to. Be prepared your arm will begin to ache after a while and if you feel a little light headed drink some water after to ground yourself.

Once you have been doing this for a while you can try finding a pendulum message board. These are available to print out on the internet or buy. Have a look around. The same rules apply with the message board but you will get far greater information and will find it is a great way to build a relationship with your guide.

How do we know if a Spirit guide is not really a guide but something malevolent?

- You're the only person the spirit has ever contacted, you are a special soul and they will only share their message with you because of this.

- Your guide talks about secret doorways to other worlds that only you have managed to open

- your guide does not have a problem with you bragging about your abilities and spiritual connections.

- The spirit claims to be your great protector from another spirit.

- The guide claims you to be some kind of spiritual leader or divine presence

- the information given to you is useless.

- The guide insists those in your life are against you

If you have any instances like this with your guide you need to be aware you are not dealing with a spirit guide. This is very important as Negatives will build you up and up before watching you fall! Spirit Guides will never act in this manner.

Angels

Like guides angels are watching over us. But they do play a different role. When people communicate with their spirit guides they do often mistake them for Angels and this is understandable. If you know nothing of spirit Guides then messages from any spiritual being from a higher realm would seem like an angel. But they are very different indeed. Angels have not lived a Human life. They are neither male or female but rather pure beings of Light. Many believe that if an Angel manifests before us it has to take another form so that we can comprehend them. Their energy alone is that powerful.

Spirit guides work kind of like the middle men, they answer to the Angels. We can work with Angels of course however these amazing beings of light tend to work with us more often on the major incidents rather than the every day.

This doesn't mean that they are not watching over you because they are and you can have every faith in this and when you call on them they will always listen. One thing many people don't realize though is that We do have to face certain trials and obstacles in order for us to complete our life path. These could be truly horrific and awful situations. When these occur some people maybe inclined to say where were the Angels then?....this is when some difficulties come in and people lose their faith because they do not understand exactly the situation regarding their life path and the missions they must complete. It is during these times that are angels are with us. They offer a warm strong embrace of safety and love. But when people begin to lose that faith in the Angels they are in a sense turning their back on their embrace and so cannot receive all the help needed. So it is important to remember whatever has happened or gone wrong your Angels are always there for you and always will be and they can only assist us if we ask them too because they cannot interfere with Free will and the course of our life path..

There are different Angels with different roles to play and they can be found in the hierarchy of Angels.

The Hierarchy of Angels

There are nine orders of Angels and these are
arranged in order of importance as follows :
Seraphim, Cherubim, Thrones, Domination's,
Virtues,Powers,Principalities, Archangels and
Angels.

These Orders are called choirs and are divided
into three triads. The Highest being the first triad
and the Lowest being the Third.

The first Triad.

Choir One – Seraphim's

The Seraphim's are the highest order of angels
and are spiritual beings of Pure Light. The Main
function of the Seraphim is to stop all negative
energies from entering the Divine energy. It is
highly unlikely that a human will ever see A
seraphim due to their Brilliant Light that is
beyond human comprehension. However we can
Ask these Angels for guidance regarding Major

Planetary events and for the good of humanity as a whole.

Choir two - Cherubim

The Cherubim are the second highest order of angels and are known as the angels of Love and wisdom. Their main function is to channel any negative energy away from the divine and also to guard places of worship as well as the light and stars. They are great protectors. We can call on them for this protection and when we are seeking their wisdom.

Choir three – Thrones

the thrones are the third highest order of Angels. These are the Angels of justice. With their may eyes they see all. When we are struggling with relationships we can look to the thrones for guidance.

The Second Triad.

Choir One – The Dominions

The Dominions are the fourth highest order of angels and are those who Watch over the universal Law of cause and effect. Ready to step in when needed to make adjustments or changes regarding major issues in politics and world rule. These are leaders and have a great and vast wisdom that we may call on when required.

Choir Two – The Virtues

The Virtues are the fifth highest order of Angela and are those that help the people who go that extra mile. The visionaries who have pushed themselves to accomplish great things may have had assistance from the virtues. Guiding us to make the seemingly impossible well within our grasp if its directed towards the higher good of all. These Angels will assist you in finding that positive drive.

Choir Three - The Powers

The Powers are The Sixth highest order of angels and they can bring justice and chaos upon our earth. They will also defend by offering you messages or a heads up when danger approaches. The powers are also the keepers of human history. We can call on these angels when we need to Defend ourselves.

The Third Triad

Choir One – The Principalities

The Principalities are the Seventh highest order of angels and they are the Guardians of vast lands and communities. They will work towards uniting humanity by channeling positive energy. When we feel our human rights are in question we can call upon these Angels.

Choir Two – The Arch Angels

The Arch Angels are the eighthe highest order of Angels and are the angels who can move between the different Levels f the Hierarchy structure. Each individual Angel in this Choir has a different purpose. They are Ruling Angels who like to be in contact with humans.

Choir Three - Angels

Finally we have the Angels. The ninth and lowest order. But by no means least. When we think of guardian angels or Angels that are each assigned a human to watch over this is the choir where we find them. These are the great messengers and go betweens. Communicating with all levels of angels. These angels will be there when we need them regarding Our births, deaths and major changes within our path. They will also protect and defend you when called upon or asked to do so.

Communicating with our Angels

Much the same as communicating with our guides Opening up to Angelic assistance is not a difficult process if we are receptive to it and it is in learning how are angels offer guidance and support in our daily lives that is important. We are all different and may find our angels work very differently with each person. We all have different personalities, Jobs, families and life situations, so it makes sense that our angels will communicate with us on a level that is in keeping with our lives and the manner in which we think. So be free to explore and discover your angels when opening up to them they are there for you and wont make it a difficult process.

One of the ways you can ask your Angels for guidance or a simple yes no question is the white Feather. This is a well known practice when communicating with our angels and it is so simple. As with all our work with the angels all you need to do is ask. This doesnt mean "Angels please grant me the lottery numbers so I can be rich" as I said before it doesn't work like that unfortunately. But they will assist you were its truly needed. Remember this when working with spirit they and your guides will only help you with what is needed to fulfill your life path and this isn't necessarily what you want. Need and want are two very different things. If something is on your mind and you need clarification ask your angels for a feather. All you need to do is tell them your question and ask " can I have a feather to clarify this please" and keep the thought or question in the back of your mind. You will receive a white feather normally within a 24 hr period for clarification. I have kept every white feather I have received as this is a gift from the divine and should be treated so. Your feather will come to you, possibly when you least expect and it will e directed to you so that you know it is for you and you alone. These gifts can bring us great comfort and a huge uplifting experience when we feel loss of direction or that we are alone. Remember after asking your angels to always thank them and again when you receive your feather.

The key element when working with our angels is to ask, they cannot help unless you do, and it is also understanding that some situations on our path we have to face and over come. This is the trouble with our life path and free will. Obstacles are sent to us to challenge and for us to over come. If the Angels stepped in with everything it could hinder our growth and we wont learn the required lesson. Rest assured when we do come across these testing times

Our angels have not deserted us and is then that they give us strength and offer guidance the most if we are open to receive.

Talk to your angels, Let them know you are aware of their presence and are greatful. You do not need fancy ritual to communicate with your angels just openness and faith that they are there and as with all tings all you need do is calm your mind and look within.

Working with Nature

Nature is a gift to us all, the energy that emanates from her is so powerful and majestic it is such a shame that so many of us do not appreciate her splendor. Simply by stepping into the back garden you enter a world of majestic beauty and powerful divine qualities which are taken for granted every day. There are many beliefs that do acknowledge this splendor with respect and courtesy. Shamanism and paganism are two major systems who do encompass the beauty of nature. They respect nature and treat her as a sister or mother and there is much we can learn from them.

I love to work with the energize nature offers, every time I venture to a new forest, beach, cave or park I am in awe at all that is occuring around me. Noticing the little things that make this world such a fascinating place. Within nature we are given another way in which we can receive guidance, love and support. From some of the most beautiful enigmatic spirits there are. All it takes is a little respect and patience. Respect nature and her spirits and she will gift you well.

People who are drawn to the outdoors and the spiritual path often begin their journey seeking out such systems as shamanism. Beginning full of enthusiasm and eagerness about studying these magical systems but soon begin to drift away from them. The novelty wheres off and the disciplines become just a little too hard or they are too out of touch within their urban, modern way of life to progress. This is a huge shame and sad to see. They then feel a little lost, always wanting to build on their connection with nature but feeling they will never be a shaman so wont continue.

Any one can connect with nature, you do not need to do a distance course in shamanism to communicate and open up to the energize that surround you. This is your birthright. Just don't over complicate the practice and you will be granted much.

The greatest way to open up the lines of communication with nature is simply to spend some time with her. A walk down a country lane or a day spent by a lake can be so very rewarding on all levels. Physical, metal and of course spiritual. You will find your self rejuvenated, fresh and with an inner knowing that you are alive and this life is a gift. So the first thing I would say when you want to work with nature is get out there! Appreciate this planet... Its the only one we have after all. We need to build a bond with nature to work with her on a spiritual level. Just as we do with a friend, we spend time with them, we get to know them and this is what we must do with our natural environment in order to pick up on the subtle messages she offers.

Nature Spirits

Nature spirits come in many forms. Some are friendly and more open to human contact others are not so. Either way all do require a little trust regarding their human co-inhabitants. You cannot just go barging in and say "hello, fairie folk....fancy a chat?". Because they will not reply. Why should they trust us ? Look at what we have doe to the planet ! Its full of turmoil and...concrete. We have steadily been destroying te very thing they try to protect and so because of this we need to re assure nature that we come in peace and champion her. This takes time and it takes patience.As with all strong relationships it wont be built over night. Nature as seen all the atrocities mankind as done to the earth as it made its progression, stomping on her each and every way it can and she saw all this long before you or I came along so be prepared to be a little patient initially.

As you begin your relationship with nature it is useful know exactly what spiritual beings you may come across. After all you are entering their domain now and it is only polite to be aware of whose who. Nature spirits are found in many cultures and encompass diversity and color. They can be found in Jewish, Persian, African, Egyptian and western systems the world over. It is largely perceived that Nature spirits are commanded by the lower orders of angels. With the devas being at the highest rung of the ladder. Devas are considered by many to be a part of the angels realm and their role is purely one of service to nature. They cannot be seen by the naked eye as they exist in the etheral realm. When we communicate with nature spirits it is largely done via thought form similar to that of our guides.

Many people the world over love to communicate with these spiritual beings because they often feel their energy to be gentle and soft. Which gives an impression of compassion and service.

The Realms of nature are viewed as being made up of four different elements :

- Fire
- Air
- Earth
- Water

These Four elements have nature spirits assigned to them. These spirits are the very essence of that element. They in some way or another have this element within their make up giving them a special connection. You will also find that these beings that reside amongst the elements even have some human features. Often seemingly comical or cartoonish too most people, but they are extremely powerful and should not be seen as anything less. Although these spiritual beings do reside in the etheral plain they still have many of the characteristics of a living human as well. They eat, sleep, live and die. Although granted the life span of a nature spirit is around 1000 years.

The Nature spirits of fire are called Salamanders

Salamanders are very powerful spirits that allow fire to exist. Imagine a world without fire...well fire is down to the salamander and if they weren't around neither would fire be. So the next time you cant light a match, close your eyes and call in a salamander. These beings have been seen by a few people as little balls of light. However They do come in various shapes and sizes. The more common perspective of them though is that they look like lizard's ranging from one foot to a foot and a half long. They do have a terrible temper as well and if they are not happy with whats going on around them their behavior can be similar to an upset toddler, throwing their toys out the pram and not understanding the consequence of their actions.

The Nature spirits of air are called Sylphs

Sylphs on the other hand are highly intelligent beings that are called to the assistance of humans when there is a need for inspiration to occur. They love creativity and if you are a creative individual you may well find sylphs around you offering the gift of inspiration. Their size varies from being very small up to the size of a fully grown human. Although they live to a ripe age they still keep their young looks!

The Nature spirits of earth are called Gnomes

The Gnomes are those plucky little characters we often see in peoples gardens protecting the lawn. The garden Gnome is common place and seen everywhere. Living in the grassy meadows or mountain landscapes. These spiritual beings much like their statue counterparts have a amazing skill at standing perfectly still when required so that they can be hidden in plane sight. They are crafty and busy. In some cultures they are also thought of as a sign of good luck. Gnomes are not particularly tall, normally around 15 cm and they can always be recognized by their bright red cap.

The Nature spirits of Water are called Undines

The Undines make up the element of water, they are water Nymphs. You will find these being in pools of water located in forestry areas. These beings can often be heard singing beautiful dolcite tunes. So when you hear the running water of a pool or waterfall listen out for their enchanting song.

How to build a healthy union with Nature.

We must build this relationship, give it a good strong firm foundation in order for it to blossom into a sweet harmonious kinship. It is the little things in life that count and doing the little things brings us great reward in the union which follows as a bi product. Begin your adventure into connecting with nature by finding a spot ear your home or perhaps even in your back garden. This is a place which you are particular drawn to and can visit on a regular basis. This will become your special place, your sacred spot of idyllic bliss. Where you can go to seek refuge and wisdom from mother earth. Once you have located where you wish this place to be go thereon a calm day and take a bin bag and your journal with.

As you approach calm your mind and centre. Focus on the intention of greeting this place as a new comer. You are entering a world where you are not the native but rather an invader coming in peace.

Focus your attention to the area around and as you observe think what can I do as a gift to this sacred spot? Is there litter around ? If there is collect it and place it in your bag. Do so in a calm and pleasant manner with a half smile. Not as though you doing a chore but rather as it is something you wish to do. As you do this you may find that some birds gather or approach nervously. Just nod to them and greet them pleasantly in your mind, they may take flight. They may not all you must do is continue your clean up operation respectfully and dutiful in service to the energies that are around.

Once you feel you have honestly done all that you can find a Tree if possible or a spot where you would wish to sit. This is the spot you are drawn too. Listen to your inner voice and allow it to guide you to the right place. This is the place you will return to time and again. As you approach do so in a soft, calm, slow moving manner as if you would not want to intrude or disturb anything. In your mind ask for permission to sit and feel the sensations you are receiving. You may feel as though your being watched. This is to be expected because you probably are. When you feel or when your body is telling you its OK to sit...take a seat.

Close your eyes for a second allow the calmness of nature to approach you. Breathe in the positive...and.... out the negative be at peace with the calm tranquilness of nature. When you open your eyes allow your mind to clear and focus your attention on observation. Do not make any harsh or speedy movements you do not wish to frighten or unsettle any energize which are around simply and calmly observe. What do you see ? How do you feel ? How is the weather reacting to your presence? Is the breeze picking up ? Does it remain still and calm ? What sensations do you have ? What animals come to view ? Write down your observations in your journal.

Now close your eyes again and listen....... Listen carefully.....allow the background noise to drift away and fade. And focus on the sound on the breeze. What do you hear ? Do you here a voice? Or do you hear nothing? It doesn't matter if you do not hear anything. As we said it takes patience. Write any instances in your journal. If you do hear a voice respond in your mind in a calm respectful manner. Do not over stay your welcome. When you feel it is time to leave. Thank the spirits who are around and ask for their permission to return. Stand up and leave in a calm and respectful manner.

Try to visit the same spot 2 – 3 times a week where possible. Have set days and times sticking to them as rigidly as your life will allow. You will find simply by spending time in nature you will build the special bond required to work with her on a spiritual level. You do not need to follow rituals, you do not need to buy fancy tools, staffs or clothing.

As your bond develops you will be able to go there with a question in mind and nature will respond with a answer. Perhaps a bird will come into view who has special symbolic meaning that answers your question ? The voice on the breeze ? Or change in weather pattern? I'm not going to tell you this is the way as this is your special bond that you are building and when nature offers you guidance and messages they will be specific to you and for your interpretation. Enjoy your journey.

Another wonderful way to connect with nature and seek answers once you have built up a special bond you will find this bond carries with you everywhere. You can take a walking meditation through nature to seek answers. This is a great exercise for your mindfulness awareness and your connection to nature and interpreting the messages she offers.

• If possible take your shoes and socks off

- As you begin your walking meditation ensure you ground and protect.

- Breathe in the positive....out the negative and continue the slow steady, natural rhythmic breathing.

- Begin your walk with a calm tranquil mind allowing all thoughts that come up to drift in and away again.

- Focus on your walk, on each step how does your body feel as you walk ? How do your feet feel connecting with the environment?

- Scan your body and its movements as you walk, once you have done this raise your awareness to the beauty around

- If you are seeking guidance from spirit now is the time to bring it into the background thoughts of your mind.

- Ask in your mind " thank you my guide and the nature spirits for being here with me, I am seeking guidance regarding..........

- just continue walking and breathing slowly and steadily allowing the course of the walk to bring you the answers

- Dont actively choose directions or paths to take just walk on intuition

- Continue to do this until you receive the answer your require this may come in the form of a bird song, a cloud formation, an animal and their symbolic meaning, a change in weather, a sensation or that inner knowing. The response will be personal to you and when it comes you will know this.

- When you have completed the walking meditation thank your guide s and the spirits who helped you.

Cloud Scrying

Cloud scrying is a wonderful way that we can connect with nature and receive guidance from her and the spiritual beings that are around. You must remember as a child laying on the grass on a warm summers day, staring up at the clouds making pictures and images as they go by on the warm summer breeze. Absolutely lovely. This is something we should indulge in as adults also not only because it re awakens our inner child bringing back those memories of our youth. But it is also a way our guides and Nature spirits can give us messages of guidance and support. I love to while away the days drifting along cloud gazing and heres how you can receive signs and symbols in the sky above.

- Pick a clear day and venture outside with your journal
- Perhaps you could visit your sacred spot ?
- Remember to Ground and Protect and bring yourself into a calm state of being.
- Now in the background of your mind focus on the question that you require guidance for
- and simply gaze up at the fluffy clouds above

- notice any sensations you receive in your body and take note
- the clouds will slowly and steadily begin to form different shapes. You can draw these shapes into your book or describe them the choice is yours.
- Once you feel you have received all the information required thank you guides

When you get home look In your journal and see what you have drawn. Now think of what these signs and symbols can mean to you. What would their symbolism mean? Why would your guides give you these? If your still unsure and have access to the internet you can look up the interpretations of each symbol by others and see If those meanings have any relevance.

But remember the symbolic meaning may not have meaning now and so this is why we keep a journal so that we can go back to it at a later date. We also have to bare in mind you may think if its relevant to me why have I had to look on the internet to find its symbolism ? Well its possibly the easiest way your guides could get the message to you and they would have known you would look on the internet or elsewhere.

Try not to get to caught up In it all just remember to enjoy the experience and have fun.

When we have fun there is an awful lot we can learn.

Listen to natures heartbeat and feel her pulse within your being, when you can do this you are at one with her divine power and magnificence...you have truly been blessed.

Wandering spirits

When you open up to the spiritual forces you may well come across some wandering spirits. This can come as a shock to some people, startle and scare them. When we encounter these souls however it is normally the initial shock of experiencing the unexpected which to be honest can make you jump. Its OK to jump, if my friend came up behind me and I didn't know he was there and he shouted boo in my ear it would make me jump!

So there is no shame in that and there is no shame in feeling un nerved or a little scared. We are always afraid of what we know least about. Its in our nature and so is to be expected. But you do have nothing to fear if you do come across a poor wandering spirit.

One way in which I got over my fear was to think of them as human. Because that's exactly what they once were. The majority of humans mean you no harm while they are alive. So why after they have passed would they mean you harm then. That wouldn't make sense at all and this is how we must view them, as human just on a different plain.

There is a reason why they are here as well or why they have come to you. Not to mean you harm but possibly for your assistance or simply because they don't know where they are? Where their going or where they've been. when you start opening yourself up to the other realms you will start attracting spirit activity like a beacon when they realise you are receptive to them they are drawn to this like a moth to the flame. This activity will increase as you begin your development however will slow down over time. Spirits kinda become excited that you know they are there and so they try to get your attention, this may feel over whelming at times but it will calm down.

Another term for wandering spirits is lost souls, their not lost because they are damned their lost because that's exactly what they are....lost.

If you feel you have come into contact with one of these spirits who has crossed into our plain. Talk to them. Ask them who they are, why they are here, if you can help. Treat them as you would a living human being, because to them they may well be.

If a spirit comes to you then it is known as a intelligent spirit. It thinks and acts as we do. Can make decisions and has choice to the extent of its capabilities. Then there is a residue haunting.

These are not intelligent spirits. Trying to communicate with them is a pointless exercise and will hold no sway over any of the events that pass. when we think of residual haunting s we think of a video player playing the same recording over and over. Some believe that these are memories that have been some how absorbed by the surrounding rock, crystals or mineral and when the conditions are right these materials project that memory for all to see.

I you are interested in the paranormal and all things that go bump in the night I would recommend joining a paranormal investigation team where you can get involved and learn more about these kind of spirits. Putting yourself in a safe environment with professionals will assist you in over coming any fears.

Then if you do come across any in your day to day life you will not have that initial fear and so will be able to help or assist the spirit in crossing over to their own plain. Which is really what we should be doing as Lightworkers.

Path of Compassion

The Path of compassion is the third and final
path in towards spiritual growth for the
Lightworkers path.we cannot teach compassion.
This is something that grows within us over time
ad experience. To assist in this growth we can
learn from teachings and adapt some of our
thought process to bring us more into alignment
with a compassionate path.

We cannot force it upon ourselves either, we
are only human and to suddenly become this
perfect being sees no wrong in anyone and
floats around on a cloud of joy 24/7 would be a
bit of a unobtainable and unrealistic goal for
most of us and to be honest for many who like to
project themselves in this image. So lets be
realistic.

We are spiritual beings, but we do argue, we do
feel negative emotions and we do allow our ego
to step in and take over from time to time. This
is human nature. What we can do is our best to
over come these obstacles and live a
compassionate path to the very best of our
ability. In doing so we can remain true to ourself
rather than over night becoming someone who
we are not.

To offer compassion to others we must first learn to be compassionate to ourself. We all make mistakes, we all do things and have done things in the past which we regret. It is unhealthy to go on through life holding onto these situations and not allowing ourselves to move on. Everything starts from you. Your world around is simply a mirror image of your inner state of being. If you struggle with areas of your path that have been hard to swallow or cannot accept, you will find the same difficulties occuring around you and with others who may cross your path. So from this point accept yourself for all that you are and all that you have done.

breathe normally in with the positive out with the negative as you breathe out the negative Repeat these words in your mind :

" I have made many mistakes on my path, some I am not proud of and some I have difficulty in moving forward from. There is not much I can do now regarding these instances and so holding onto them like a weight which anchors me down is not productive either. What I can and will do is learn from these mistakes and treat them as lessons that I have learnt from along my path so that I may teach those who walk the path behind me from my mistakes and ensuring they do not suffer as I or others may have now I wish to move forward and progress". Allow the words to flow away with the out breathe.

Know in your heart that you have moved on now, you are seeking a new path and all that has gone before holds no power on the path that emerges ahead. All that it does is allows you to have a broader knowledge and experience to assist others.

We can learn much about compassion from other belief systems ad cultures. Buddhism encapsulates compassion and wisdom as the way to enlightenment. Enlightenment being reaching the pinnacle of your spiritual journey and so further reading on this beautiful system is highly recommended.

 At the end of the day however we can look else where for teachings on compassion, raise our awareness and build up a knowledge base but compassion starts from within us and we may need to develop control over our reaction and the way in which we present our emotions to others to build a stronger force of compassion.

We do this by developing a thoughtful, nurturing state of being as opposed to a reacting machine of thoughtless responses to triggers that occur throughout our path. This is not an easy process and can take a long time disciplining our selves away from the mindset we know. The way we can begin to do this is by choice.

We all have free will and choice is one of the greatest gifts we ave been given (although it can become one of our greatest enemies if not used towards the highest good of all).we need to train our mid to choose our response rather than simply reacting as we always do.

Stop, think and answer when in a debate or an argument is ensuing. Normally we simply answer rushing in to defend ourselves our actions like a Tommy gun on automatic fire. Bang ..bang ..bang ...we go and before long all we are left with is the aftermath of destruction and chaos caused largely by an unthoughtful out response and heavily armoured words that become bullets piercing the skin of our victim and penetrating their hearts.

Throughout the course of the lightworkers handbook you have been asked to calm the mind, breathe in the positive...and.... out the negative. ..this must become your reaction now. When you feel that the situation is changing and trouble may be brewing, bring your state of calm in. this is the ultimate way to defuse a situation. Even if the other party is continuing blasting you in an argument it is hard for them to continue when you receive their barrage with calmness and grace. Calm the mind and choose your response. This will become second nature over time and a thoughtful mind will develop. Allow it to come in to every situation and circumstance you encounter.

Before you respond think about your reply. Often when we have had an argument or a situation where we have not displayed our love and compassion for another or acted in a productive way we look back and regret our actions, this is the power of hindsight. We ask forgiveness and make our apologise.

All that negative energy bomb blasting around the area for nothing and you know all that negative energy has to go somewhere. So as we develop a more thoughtful mind so to our compassion for others will flourish as we grow a greater understanding of their feelings and seeing things from another's perspective.

Seeing things from another's perspective is the key to compassion.

The way of love and compassion is quite simply the True Spiritual way. When we can learn to develop the quality of love the possibilities of life really begin to unfold.

So what is love?

Love is the fruit that grows from the seed of compassion. Love is Universal and yet to many it is an alien emotion or simply just a word.

So here's an exercise imagine if we lost the word ?

If we lose the word **LOVE** in our everyday life how else can we express the emotion?

Well the only other way we can express Love without the word or label is through **ACTION** !

Seems very simple on paper, we tell our partners, husbands, wives , kids we love them everyday. But it is said so often the word becomes mangled, over used on a conveyor belt of repetition.

Which sadly makes it just a popular word rather than a meaningful one. For if a word is to have meaning it must have substance and foundation which lead to a firm solid outcome or result.

Heres an experiment :

Throughout the week ahead I would like you to observe your thoughts and speech pattern, see how many times you use the word love, measure how often we use the word compared to express the emotion.

Actions speak louder than words!

You can even try and leave out the word and express it in a productive way so someone **KNOWS** you love them by your deeds rather than voice. Try and do at least one thing each day over the next week that is purely out of love for another human being animal or plant. Im not saying don't tell your kids you love them or your spouse, just try to become more active in giving your love.

We cannot become loving or compassionate over night! But contemplating the driving force behind love and the product that ensues can help us to develop a more loving compassionate persona and way of being. Its not difficult there are no rituals to teach, no churches or temples simply allow love in.

Here is a simple meditation to begin with. This can be performed daily, weekly where ever whenever and if you have children it is also a great meditation for them to learn and begin with.

Sharing love :

- Ground and Protect

- Find a comfortable spot relax sitting or lying down which ever is best for you Close your eyes and breathe.

- Do not force the breathe or breathe in a particular manner just breathe as you would normally into a nice slow steady rhythm watching the breathe at all times.

- As you relax remember something that makes you feel happy. Think of good times you've spent with a friend or family member, a favourite past time or hobby even a child hood toy or incident that brought you joy.

- Place both of your hands on your chest as you contemplate your happy moment and imagine the feeling of warmth, peace and happiness grow from there and to all over your body.

- Imagine that the happiness you hold in your heart is now spreading out all over you and out further too your family members.

- Then out to all your friends this warm loving happiness glow of loving kindness.

- Then out to all those you work with your colleagues and those you don't know

- And slowly out to all those around the world. Reaching out the loving kindness energy which began at your chest is now touching everyone on the planet.

- All animals , plants and people.

- When your ready calmly bring yourself back with a lovely smile, try to keep this smile or half smile throughout your day.

It can be difficult wishing happiness and love to people we don't like or don't know But it is important to remember love and compassion is our universal connection that we can share with everyone and everything.

Remain True to yourself

This is the core meaning and understanding of what it is to wake up to a spiritual pathway such as Lightwork. Lightworkers are the man on the street or the woman in the park, the child at the bus stop or the elderly couple in the home. Each and every single person has it in them to switch on the button and dissolve the darkness into the light. But the term Lightworker alone gives birth to many Ego driven self empowering roles amongst us and is often used not for the good of the people or the planet but instead to massage an ego or to aid in an escape from the real world where people are needed to do real good.

Ritualistic Practice (often misinterpreted) past on by generations and generations of distant tribes and cultures fuels these egos into a hidden pretence that they are superior or more highly evolved (I have heard this many times) than others and also an awful lot of wasted energy. All the while there are True Lightworkers, those souls who have truly dedicate their life path to one of service to others go about their day without recognition, fancy ritualistic behaviour, a halo and believe it or not they don't have wings! In fact many go through their lives without a big cosmic experience, without finding out in their past life they were Cleopatra and without Jesus, Mother Theresa or Bruce lee as their Spiritual helper.

The trouble is those who are called to wake up are losing themselves amongst the mysticism and to be honest missing the point completely.

the very essence of spirituality or any spiritual journey begins with love. This is the energy needed to carry one along their path for without love there is no journey and where does the journey begin? It begins with ourself.

So in order to give love we first have to love and nurture ourself but how is that possible when we are simply living by pre - prescribed roles that became outworn aeons ago and fitted with that time and place. This is where we lose ourselves and so in turn cannot love our own true nature, our true self so how can we give love when this occurs? Although we may think we do. But this is simply a masquerade.

We can learn from the ways of old and cultures far and wide, shamans, priestesses,Monks etc. that is great and wonderful to learn from, pass on and experience. if love is to carry you on your journey allow knowledge to hold each of your hands to support and guide you. But it is that fine line which causes us to drift from our true path and from being our true self. People are so concerned about whether they are a label the issues they should be dealing with are falling by the way side, relationships suffer and ultimately so does their life path.

Why? OK we've spent a long time searching for our label (wasted time) then we join others and converse about how much love we have and what we can do (each trying to sound more in touch with the divine than the next wasting more time and energy) until the novelty wears off.....and we find some new label...then we begin again.

Sticks and stones may break my bones but names will never hurt me...no they wont ..and they wont put you any more in tune with your higher self and ultimately with your life path either.

WAKE UP!

You know you have a purpose in this life, you know deep down your connection to others is strong, your bond with the earth is beautiful and your natural empathic qualities are overwhelming. Tune them by using them and use them for the very reason you were given them not to become the next T.V. Psychic, You Tube levitating Shaman Or God forbid Egotistical Cult leader. Start living now in this moment, in this life, in this skin. This is the moment and you are the individual who will make a difference to many people on your path by simply living with love as your vehicle.

I Have this short story to share with you :

There was once a man named Tim. Tim lived his life searching for a purpose or higher worth, This made his life his true self feel dull, uninteresting and with loss of direction.

Until he decided to seek out his spiritual journey. Buddhism seemed to be trending at the time on the internet so Tim saw this as a sign. Feeling drawn to this magical way of life Tim began to make his way to the book shop with the intention of finding some guidance regarding his path.

As he walked down the road he noticed an old man pushing his car up the hill with his wife behind the wheel. Tim saw this and considered helping when a man came along and started pushing, when this happened Tim said oh good cos I don't have time and crossed the road, continuing on his journey Tim then witnessed someone being mugged oh my God he thought but what can I do im a pasethist turning the other cheek Tim darted down an alley out the way and said in his mind ill put a bubble of love around that poor person and my guides will help her.

Then he came to the shop as he entered he passed a homeless man on the street who asked him to buy the Big issue. Tim just Said sorry I have no change and ran into the shop. When Tim re-emerged he darted back home to read the two books he had bought at £19.99 each. He shaved his head,Became Vegetarian, he read his books and he carried out the mantras daily for a couple of weeks.....but felt nothing...he was still Tim. He switched on his computer hoping to see more articles about mantras, the Dalai lama and such but instead what was trending on the internet now was very different

....OLD Man has heart attack while thief offers help then steals pensioners wallet while he pushes his car. The old man dies shortly after in Hospital......

...... if bystanders had called police when lady was being mugged in full view killer would not have killed second victim .....

........Ex soldier found Homeless and dead in book shop doorway, cold, malnourished and alone. Reports say he was last seen selling Big issue.......

These are all instances that do not need mantras, crystals, rituals, cosmic alliance, fasting or higher wisdom. These are all instances where Tim could have made a difference in that moment and the repercussions of him not simply rippled.

Tim still felt empty after reading his books, Tim isn't a Buddhist monk, He is Tim and its Tim who could have made a difference to many peoples lives in one trip to the shop.

So Imagine what we could do in an entire life time by being our True self.

Sometimes people lose their true purpose trying to be the label instead of living the path, Which is an awful shame for that person. Don't fall into that trap.

The Lightworkers path is one riddled with excitement, challenges, joy and tears.

I wish you well on your journey my friend.

Love and Light

XXX

7321100R0

Made in the USA
Charleston, SC
17 February 2011